No person in the United States shall, on the basis of sex, be excluded from participation in, be denied the benefits of, or be subjected to discrimination under any education program or activity receiving Federal financial assistance.

-TITLE IX OF THE U.S. EDUCATION AMENDMENTS, JUNE 23, 1972

This group is so resilient, is so tough, has such a sense of humor. It's just so badass. There's nothing that can faze us. . . . We have pink hair and purple hair, we have tattoos and dreadlocks. We got white girls and black girls . . . straight girls and gay girls. I couldn't be more proud of this team.

-MEGAN RAPINOE, JULY 10, 2019

PRIDE
— OF A —
NATION

A Celebration of the U.S. Women's National Soccer Team

FOREWORD BY JULIE FOUDY
ESSAYS BY GWENDOLYN OXENHAM

EDITED BY DAVID HIRSHEY, ROGER DIRECTOR, AND ROB FLEDER

AN OFFICIAL U.S. SOCCER BOOK

TEN SPEED PRESS
California | New York

CONTENTS

BAND OF SI

BY JULIE FOUDY

THE HALL OF FAMER AND FORMER COCAPTAIN OF THE FABLED 99ERS DESCRIBES WHAT IT TOOK FOR THE U.S. WOMEN TO GATE-CRASH THE NATIONAL CONSCIOUSNESS AND THE CHALLENGES AHEAD FOR THE NEXT GENERATION OF CHAMPIONS.

WE WAITED our whole lives for this moment—the first Women's World Cup to be held on American soil—and we wanted to set a standard, a benchmark for every World Cup to follow. We wanted big stadiums, a national footprint, large crowds, lots of buzz. The only question was kinda important: Could we fill these big stadiums? The players, of course, immediately thought, "Oh hell, yes," and a year in advance we had already set our sights. We hit the road, doing autograph sessions, clinics, appearances, any and all events to drive publicity and attention to our World Cup journey.

Cut to Nike headquarters in Portland, Oregon. Nike is staging the opening ceremony for their newest and largest building on campus. The entire team was invited because the building bore a special dedication. . . . It was the Mia Hamm Building. Which was mildly ironic, considering that if you were to look for Mia, the last place you'd find her was in the spotlight. Nevertheless, the rest of us were ecstatic that we got to celebrate our star teammate in such a singular moment. Knowing how much she "loved" the attention, we labeled every item in our hotel: The Mia Hamm Pillow. The Mia Hamm Door. You get the gist. When Mia walked into the hotel and saw our handiwork she just shook her head and giggled.

→
The ESPN broadcaster is as relaxed and articulate in the studio as she was intense and vocal on the field, where she was known as "Loudy Foudy."

STERS

If the USWNT were a drink, I would say, pour one part fully committed to one part ridiculous and add a splash of nasty.

Enshrined in the National Soccer Hall of Fame on the same day (August 26, 2007), Foudy and Mia Hamm are among the owners of the NWSL's new Angel City FC franchise.

THAT WAS OUR U.S. TEAM. Equal parts intense and bat-shit silly. If the USWNT were a drink, I would say, pour one part fully committed to one part ridiculous and add a splash of nasty. When you understand that about us, you start to appreciate that our journey wasn't just about the hardware. Yes, accolades are more than welcome because teams are typically measured in medals and championships. Legacies are often linked to titles. And we've collected quite a haul. This U.S. Women's Team, over the course of its history dating back to the 1980s, has won four World Cups and 4 Olympic gold medals for a total of eight world titles. That's more than twice as many as the next closest country, Germany (but who's counting?). So please don't get me wrong, we love the bling and winning has always been the goal for this team. It's just never been the focus.

For generation after generation, the focus has always been on creating a family, competing our butts off, having fun, making our country proud, and thinking bigger than sports. The formula is pretty simple really. Create and sustain a culture that values the we, the sisterhood, and the possible, treating the podium as not just a place to celebrate but also a platform from which to holler for the world to up its game.

And holler we did. We never had a shortage of feisty women with great vocal chords, willing to use them. Maybe that should have been apparent way, way back in 1985 when the first USWNT to travel abroad did their pre-game cheer, straight from the soul: OOSA OOSA OOSA UHHHHHH. As the story goes, that's how the fans in the stadium in Jesolo, Italy, pronounced the name of our country which they saw on the jerseys and the scoreboard. The U.S. players thought it was cool and made it their own. To this day, what started with that original team fittingly still roars out in the pregame huddle of every USWNT game.

AHHH, THE 80S, when the U.S. National Team was formed, a glorious era with its wonderfully cringy trappings: big hair, mullets (Mia "business in the front, party in the back" Hamm), scrunchies (Carla Overbeck was the queen of these), *Flashdance* off-the-shoulder sweatshirts with a sports bra (looking at you, Brandi Chastain), VHS tapes to watch game film, Kristine Lilly's yellow Sony Walkman cassette player, which I thought was perhaps the coolest thing I had ever seen. We were just a bunch of kids (literally: Mia was fifteen, I was sixteen, and Kristine Lilly was sixteen), incredibly grateful to be playing for our country, and completely clueless as to what that meant. There were no World Cups or Olympics for women's soccer back in the 80s, although there had been for men's soccer since the 1900 Olympics and the 1930 World Cup. Why, you ask? Because we were told it's not what women do. Besides, people won't come to see you play. Well, as you can imagine, that didn't go over well with this group of women. The USWNT players think people care about women's soccer. Just you watch.

There was sufficient hollering by enough players and advocates of the women's game for FIFA to say OK, OK, we will give you your first Women's World Cup, we are just not sure we will call it a World Cup yet. Hence the title: The M&M Mars Cup (I wish I was joking). It was to be staged in China in the fall of 1991, and I remember telling my parents, "Mom! Dad! You are not going to believe it. We are finally going to get to play in our first Women's World Cup and it's in China." Now mind you, my parents were incredibly supportive of my soccer career but not exactly steeped in the hallowed history of the game. So maybe I shouldn't have been surprised by my father's reaction to the groundbreaking news: "Oh Julie, I am not sure I can make it, as that is a really busy time for me work-wise."

"Dad, this is kinda a big deal," I explained. "World Cups happen only once every four years. I may never make it to another. And this is the first ever for women. And you're gonna be there, Dad." I always giggle out loud when I think of that exchange. Imagine a parent of one of today's players saying, Sorry honey, I don't think I can make that World Cup, and what in the heck is a World Cup anyway?

↑ Never one to shirk a demanding challenge, Foudy here muscles her way past a German defender in the semifinals of the 2004 Olympics.

↓ Standing for more than just excellence on the field, USWNT players (from left) Megan Rapinoe, Margaret Purce, Crystal Dunn, and Catarina Macario take a knee in support of the Black Lives Matter movement before a game against Canada in 2021.

JUST GOES TO SHOW YOU how much this game has grown here in the U.S. (or perhaps how oblivious my folks were). Part of me yearns for those early days of playing and the simplicity of it all. I remember never taking my cleats off after games as a wee lass. I'd wear them everywhere until I wore the studs down to just stubs. I'm not sure of the exact day I fell under the spell of soccer, but the smell of fresh-cut grass, the laughter of a group of rad girls, and the freedom to compete without judgment had me at the first kick. We were just playing because it made our hearts happy, and it felt good. And that spell has been a strong, gorgeous one. I've either been playing the game, broadcasting the game, teaching the game, or admiring the game my entire life.

↑ At camps and clinics, such as Foudy's Leadership Academy, the 99ers continue to build their legacy by passing their love of the game along to young girls.

→ On October 27, 2015, President Barack Obama invited the 2015 World Cup winners to the White House, where he lauded the strides made by female athletes, proclaiming that "playing like a girl means you're a badass."

But back to my folks. To be fair to Slim Jim and Fruity Judy, we never had women's soccer role models back in the day. Nor did we have national teams or World Cups or Olympics to showcase them. As my friend and mentor Billie Jean King once pointed out to me, "We were the first generation in tennis, you all are the first gen in soccer. The first gens set all the standards and the culture," she said.

"They also go through all the shit," I added, laughing. "But it is the shit that makes you great." I really believe that. Perspective, the gift that keeps on giving. What I didn't realize is that future generations would also have to overcome obstacles. Whether it was for equitable treatment back in the '90s or the more recent equal-pay fight of this current team, we continue to holler while on top of podiums. Our goal is twofold: to leave the game in a better place for the next generation and to be an inspiration for all seeking equal rights. That was a vital lesson I also learned from Billie Jean King when I first met her in the early '90s and we spoke about the lack of support for the women's game: "Foudy, what are you as players doing about it? You. What are you all doing? Speak up. Stand up. You have the power." You're damn right we do. And we have made it our mission for the next generations to understand that as well. I'd say mission accomplished! This current group, as we all know, grabbed that baton and didn't stop sprinting until they reached the historic legal settlement in which U.S. Soccer pledged equal compensation for its men's and women's teams going forward. And that gets right to the heart of all I love and cherish about this USWNT year after year, decade after decade. We care deeply . . . about each other, about the game, about society, about being both inspirational and aspirational. The USWNT has spent its entire history making courage contagious. I could not be prouder to be part of this amazing sisterhood. May you be equally inspired by this book. OK then, here we go, before our next adventure . . . give it from deep within your soul, all together now: OOSA OOSA OOSA UHHHH.

The USWNT has spent its entire history making courage contagious. I could not be prouder to be part of this amazing sisterhood.

1980S

WITH A BALL
AND A DREAM,
A GROUP OF
TOUGH-MINDED,
SOCCER-LOVING
WOMEN CAME
TOGETHER IN 1985
TO FORM THE
FIRST-EVER
NATIONAL TEAM.

←
The U.S. Women defeated Brazil, China, and Japan to advance to the 1986 "Mundialito" final in Jesolo, Italy. Here, they relax between games. Back row (left to right): Gretchen Gegg, Janine Sparza, Emily Pickering, April Heinrichs, Marsha McDermott, Debbie Belkin, Joan Dunlap, Cindy Gordon; middle row: Chris Tomek, Kim Crabbe, Michelle Akers; front row: Lisa Gmitter, Stacey Enos, Betsy Drambour.

THE PIONEERS

BY GWENDOLYN OXENHAM

↑ The poster for the "Little World Cup," pitting the U.S. against more seasoned teams—Italy, Denmark, and England.

AT THE OPENING ceremony of the 1985 National Sports Festival in Baton Rouge, Louisiana, diver Greg Louganis carries the torch as fireworks explode in the sweltering night sky. The 55,000 fans filling LSU's Tiger Stadium are there to watch the top amateur athletes in the U.S. compete against one another—and among them are seventy of the country's best women soccer players. There's a feeling in the air: Something is brewing.

At the festival's end, officials announce that a national team is forming. They call out seventeen names. Every player sitting in the grass hopes to hear her name.

There is no women's soccer in the Olympics yet. There is no women's World Cup. But that stops no one from dreaming.

These pioneers—most of whom you've never heard of—start everything, playing in an era when you still had to hand back your USA gear after each trip.

Their stories hinge on grit: They follow this game anywhere. Take Emily Pickering, a self-described "poor kid" from Long Island. She would lose her brother to a drunk driver when she was six; in high school, her best friend died in a car accident while sitting next to her. The game was what Pickering had. Her high school coach drove her nine hours to Chapel Hill because UNC was one

←
The original USWNT were winless in their inaugural 1985 tournament in Jesolo, but they laid the groundwork for the future glory of the team.

↓ "She was a vicious tackler and had tremendous pace," says U.S. coach Anson Dorrance of Kim Crabbe, whom he called up to the National Team after watching her lead George Mason University to the 1985 NCAA championship over his North Carolina Tar Heels.

of the few schools with scholarships. That audition changed her life. "She was a frigging ass kicker," says UNC coach Anson Dorrance. "She was the alpha."

Kim Crabbe, the first Black player ever called up to the National Team, describes her single mother as her "forever hero." While her mom worked three jobs to support the family, Kim's favorite youth coach, Mr. Fox, gave her rides to games in his red VW bus. Her aunt, dubbed "Lil' Feisty," also played—well into her sixties—and came to her niece's games. "If someone made a choice comment—especially about a teammate of color—Auntie was the one who set them straight," says Crabbe.

Lisa Gmitter, a Jersey girl, won the first collegiate Player of the Year award in 1985 after her George Mason team beat UNC to win the NCAA championship. She has a dozen notebooks full of memories: borrowing a bicycle from a stranger because she was late to a banquet in China; cutting her teammates' hair as the unofficial team barber; scoring a goal against Sweden; ordering pizza with her fifteen-year-old roommate, Mia Hamm.

Lori Henry was a three-year captain of the USWNT who shouted curse words on the field so often that the coaches implemented a no-swearing rule. Joan Dunlap scored the 1981 National Championship-winning penalty kick for her amateur team, the Seattle Sharks, when she was five months pregnant; two years later, she got a full ride to UNC and brought her toddler with her. Margaret "Tucka" Healy entered UC Berkeley in 1981; the school didn't offer scholarships, but when she graduated, her coach gave her five hundred dollars for a plane ticket to Germany so she could continue playing. Pickering quit her payroll job to go play for Juventus in Italy. Forward Shannon McMurty went to play in Australia. But many of the older players eventually asked themselves: *How long before I start my life?* Without a way of making a living from soccer in the United States, the women began to move on. Healy remembers standing on the field during a corner kick in the middle of a club game, looking at her teammates in uniform, and thinking, *What am I still doing out here?* After that she only played for fun. "It was not easy to quit," says Healy. She became employee number 81 at a little start-up company in Mountain View called Google. "My experience with the National Team taught me to be early and first—and that I loved being at the beginning of things," says Healy. Cindy Gordon, a scrappy forward, would become a scientist at a biomedical genetics lab. Goalkeeper Kim Wyant went on to become the head coach of NYU's men's soccer team—one of only two women coaching men in the NCAA.

Many of these women have stayed in the game—Crabbe now runs a free youth city league for at-risk kids in Wilmington and was named U.S. Soccer Coaches' 2021 Youth Coach of the Year. After the local news ran a story about Crabbe, her players stared up at her, a touch aggrieved. "Why," they asked, "didn't you tell us who you are?" Now they know: Their coach is one of the originals—a trailblazer for the millions of dreamers to come.

1990s

THE U.S. WOMEN REPRESENTED A COUNTRY THAT DIDN'T KNOW WHO THEY WERE OR WHAT GAME THEY WERE PLAYING. BUT BY DECADE'S END, THEY HAD WON THE HEARTS AND MINDS OF A NATION AND REVOLUTIONIZED WOMEN'S SPORTS FOREVER.

→
Surrounded by Norwegian defenders, Michelle Akers skies to head the ball during the USWNT's 2-1 victory in the 1991 World Cup final in China.

All aboard for the USWNT in Port-au-Prince, Haiti, as the team begins the long journey toward the inaugural 1991 World Cup to be played later that year in China.

OOSA: THE BEGINNING

BY GWENDOLYN OXENHAM

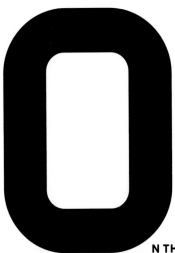

N THE EDGE of the Venetian lagoon in the beach town of Jesolo, Italy, the quaint, 4,000-capacity stadium is full, crackling and alive with Italian fans who have come to see the *Mundialito*—that's Spanish for "Little World Cup," and the title of the original global-invitational tournament for women.

Many fans think the story of the U.S. Women's National Team starts in 1991, but it begins earlier—in August 18, 1985. And everything that the USWNT has achieved in its paradigm-shifting history started with the initial step they took off the bus to play their first international match. As the Americans, including a lion-haired nineteen-year-old named Michelle Akers, walk through the tunnel to the field, their senses are going wild: It's a brilliant sunny day, you can smell the Adriatic Sea, and little bits of mysterious paper rain down on them. They hear a hum, a chant, low and constant, almost like the sound of cicadas, defender

Stacey Enos recalls. OOSA. OOSA. OOSA. At first the Americans believe they're being booed—*oh my god, they hate us*, Enos thinks. When she looks up at the sea of faces above her to see whether the Italians fans are *actually* throwing things at them, she glimpses the barista she has befriended—the teenager she orders a cappuccino from every morning. He grins at her and his voice emerges from the low drone around him, breaking that steady rhythm, as he shouts: OOSA, OOSA. And that's when Enos realizes that the confetti-throwing *calcio* fans are in fact cheering for them, blending the USA letters into one chantable word; they are encouraging the Americans.

As the team lines up at midfield, the "Star-Spangled Banner" begins to play over the loudspeaker. They'd sung the anthem days earlier at practice. Coach Mike Ryan, a Seattle steelworker and longtime youth coach, had brought out a boom box. They'd all belted out the words. Now, as they turn toward the flag and sing—*O say can you see, by the dawn's early light*—they fully understand what this moment means: They are the first American women to play for their country; they are the great beginning.

When the starting eleven huddle up at midfield, Enos looks into the faces of her teammates and grins: Oosa. They pile their hands on top of each other. Instead of saying, "One, two, three, USA," they shout, "OOSA, OOSA, OOSA." This is what the U.S. Women will shout in every pregame huddle from then on—an adrenaline-inducing homage to those first pioneers.

THE AMERICANS do not win a single game in Jesolo in 1985. They'd practiced together for less than *five* days. The other teams are more experienced, their style more sophisticated. They also come from soccer-steeped countries. For the Americans, the game was not inherited. It was found. The Americans have done whatever they needed to do to keep playing in a country that doesn't love the sport the way they do. Yes, they lose to the Italians—but not by much. And now they are hungry to win.

The next year in Jesolo, 1986, they have a new coach, Anson Dorrance, who dropped out of UNC law school to coach the Tar Heels soccer teams. Under Dorrance, the UNC women have won four of the first five national titles. He will go on to win more national titles (twenty-two) than any coach in any collegiate sport in history. In Jesolo that year the Americans finish second—they are off to the races. Over the next

In China, the U.S. outscores opponents 25-5. They are the only team to play with three forwards—Carin Jennings, April Heinrichs, and Michelle Akers, whom the Chinese press dub the "Triple-Edged Sword."

→ Mia Hamm enjoys some downtime circa 1992 with her teammates at the University of North Carolina, which went undefeated and won four national championships while she was there. Left to right: Angela Kelly, Hamm, Tisha Venturini, and Kerri Sanchez.

→ Michelle Akers, the physically imposing future USWNT legend, lashes a shot against Brazil en route to a 5-0 rout in an opening-round 1991 World Cup match in Guangzhou City.

five years, they come together for weeks at a time, traveling around the world—from Cyprus to Trinidad—to play other national teams. In 1987, the U.S. team becomes some of the first Americans allowed into China, "kingdom of bicycles." Millions cycle through the city boulevards. The team takes a seventeen-hour coal train ride through the countryside in the heat, windows down, and by the time they get there, their faces are so smudged with ash they look like chimney sweeps. At the open-air markets, they notice the hanging hogs' heads and gleefully buy one—then they sneak into Anson's bathroom, wedge it into his toilet bowl, face up, and put the lid down. "We were hoping it would scare the crap out of him," says Carla Overbeck.

In Portugal, huddled around a long wooden table, they play the card game spoons: First person to get four of the same suit of cards sneakily snatches one of the spoons and waits for someone to notice, then all hell breaks loose as everyone else lunges, fights, and claws to get one of the remaining spoons. "That game always ended with bloody knuckles," Overbeck recalls. In Italy, on off days, they ride mopeds through wine country. In Sardinia, they practice on a gravel field that grinds their cleats flat. In Haiti, when there's no hot water, they bathe in the hotel swimming pool. During the power blackouts, they spend hours reading by candlelight, passing books around to fill the time. The college players—Julie Foudy (Stanford)—Mia Hamm and Kristine Lilly (UNC), return to school with wax drippings on their textbooks.

These years of shared experiences in far-flung corners of the world—back in a time when you still spun a globe to see where you were going—create the team culture: They are appreciative and they are tough. They are friends for life. And they like to win—preferably in a stylish, spectacular way, scoring showers of beautiful goals.

IN 1991, the United States plays in the "FIFA World Championship for Women's Football for the M&Ms Cup" in China. This is the first women's world championship sanctioned by FIFA, the sport's international governing body, although FIFA is unwilling to christen the event an official "World Cup" in case the event turns out a failure. But it isn't a failure: China fills the stadiums and the whole country follows along.

In China, the U.S. outscores opponents 25-5. They are the only team to play with three forwards on their frontline—Carin Jennings, April Heinrichs, and Michelle Akers, who the Chinese press dub the "Triple-Edged Sword."

Jennings has a ponytail that Chinese fans—who have never seen a blond in person—keep reaching over to touch. That ponytail whips behind her as she streaks and cuts down the field, exceptional with the ball at her feet.

Akers looks like a Roman statue come to life, tall, strong, and chiseled, with dramatic cheekbones. Her Mufasa nickname isn't just because of her mane; she also has a lion's majesty. Her teammates speak of her with awe. Powerful and precise, a force in the air, a winner who can orchestrate the entire midfield, she is described by her teammates as the best of all time.

They play a unique, high-pressure style. People regularly speak of the "winning American mentality," an imbued grit, and it's possible that idea is born from this applied pressure: As soon as the other team's defenders receive the ball, the Americans charge at you, storming you, stripping dazed opponents of the ball before they understand what's happening. In the quarterfinals against Chinese-Taipei, Akers scores five goals; in the semifinal against powerhouse Germany, Gabarra scores three. And in front of 65,000 fans in Guangzhou for the final, Akers scores two more to carry the Americans to a 2-1 victory over Norway.

Carin Jennings leaves the German goalkeeper and a defender sprawled on the field while scoring in the 1991 World Cup semifinal that the U.S. goes on to win 5-2.

↑ In the first ever Olympic competition for women's soccer, Mia Hamm turns on the afterburners and races past a helpless Chinese goalkeeper during the Americans' 2-1 gold medal victory in Athens, Georgia, in 1996.

Hundreds of Chinese fans flock toward the Americans, holding up notepads toward the open windows of their retro bus, begging for the signatures of the team that has—in the six years since their debut in Jesolo—become the best in the world.

Not that you'd have known of their dominance in America. In the U.S., the games are only shown on an obscure television station in the middle of the night due to the time zone difference from China. The players return to anonymity. The young players, benefactors of one life-altering piece of legislation, Title IX, go back to college soccer programs. The other players return to day jobs. Jennings—who won the Golden Ball in China, the award for player of the tournament—is unemployed. Before the World Cup, when she'd asked for time off from her marketing job so that she could go, her employer said no. *Welp, looks like it's time to quit another job, Carin,* her teammates had said with a clap on her shoulder. *We need ya.* Now the tournament is over, and there is no plan for them, no way to make a living from soccer. The team plays in occasional games that fans don't know about. When Brandi Chastain's mom, a former cheerleader, brought a megaphone out to the field, an embarrassed Brandi said, "Mom—there's like a dozen fans here—you don't need that thing, I can hear you just fine!"

In the quiet, the players train and play and grow. Behind that Triple-Edged Sword of veterans, there are the youngsters who will become defining figures in American soccer folklore.

On the right wing, there's Mia Hamm. Several years earlier, Dorrance had stood on a sideline scouting her, feeling a little ridiculous to have flown all the way to Texas to watch a fourteen-year-old. But then he saw her run. He knew which one she was without asking. For the rest of his life, any time he recounts that first time seeing her, he describes her in the same way: "She looked like she was shot out of a cannon." She flies at goal with an insistency, an inevitability, a desperation. In her big brown eyes, you can see the want. "Mia *had* to score goals," says Dorrance. "If she didn't, she was miserable, wrecked. Not too many players out there have that level of downright *need*—as well as the talent and speed to make it happen." She would move from midfield to forward and score a hundred international goals by the time she was twenty-six.

Foudy has a SoCal, just-out-of-the-waves ease to her: a laidback, slightly mischievous smile; a playful assuredness. But on the field, she has the same quality they all have: urgency.

Beside her is Julie Foudy, an entirely different ethos. Foudy has a SoCal, just-out-of-the-waves ease to her: a laidback, slightly mischievous smile; a readiness to crack a joke; a playful assuredness. But on the field, she has the same quality they all have: urgency. She is graceful but emphatic. A touch more relaxed on the field than Mia, not quite as desperate. She has a midfielder's wider curiosity for the angles and situations around her, while Mia is always looking for only one: the fastest way to goal. And Foudy has the vision to find her in those dangerous spaces and get her the ball.

Kristine Lilly, who will play for the USWNT for twenty-three years, is crafty and skillful, and also scrappy and relentless. Maybe of all of them, she's the one who loves the game the most. Long after her teammates retire, she stays out there. She would go on to play more international games—354—than any man or woman in global history.

Behind them, like Foudy, Joy Fawcett also has that California glide—her play so simple and smooth it takes a while for Dorrance to pick up on how good she is. Off the field, she is modest, kind. In 1994, when she has a baby, she does so with that same unassuming humility, like it's no big deal—even though no player of her era had done this before.

And then there's Carla Overbeck, the bastion of calm authority. Cool but stoically fierce. "First time I saw her, I was afraid of her," says Julie Foudy. She becomes the center back and the captain for the next ten years. Following in Joy's footsteps, she too has a baby. When the team travels, opponents stare in awe, goo and gah, and then pull them aside to ask for advice—*How did you pull it off? Did your body change? Did your coach support you? How did you get your federation to pay for a nanny? How does it work?* "At banquets, the Chinese team would always ask if they could hold the kids—Joy was more hesitant but I was always like, 'Here ya go,' and I'd hand Jackson right over and then have to find him at the end of the banquet," says Overbeck with a laugh. The kids go with them on the trips; they are in the hotel rooms and on the sidelines; they are part of the adventure.

↑ The architects of the early American dynasty: Anson Dorrance (top), coach of the '91 champions, and Tony DiCicco (bottom), who guided the 99ers to glory.

↑ Shannon MacMillan gives the U.S. the early lead in the 1996 Olympic gold medal game against China, which the U.S. wins 2-1 before 76,481 fans at Sanford Stadium in Athens, Georgia.

THE 1995 WORLD CUP is not what they hoped it would be. Instead of the enormous crowds from China, there are only a few thousand people in the stands in Sweden; it feels more like the quaint summer-festival atmosphere back in Jesolo. Akers, the team's heartbeat, gets hurt in the first game. In the semifinal, the Americans fall to their Norwegian rivals 1-0. After the game, the Norwegians celebrate by crawling on all fours around the field, holding on to the ankles of the player in front of them: a victory train. Which feels to the Americans a whole lot like their nemesis is rubbing the result in their faces. Goalkeeper Briana Scurry makes herself watch: "I wanted to burn that image into my brain and onto my heart and use it to make sure it never happened again."

A year later, in 1996, women's soccer is, for the first time, in the Olympics. Hosted in Atlanta, the players know this is their chance to burst into public consciousness. In game one, more than 25,000 fans watch the U.S. pound Denmark 3-0. By the semis, that sea of fans with painted faces and handmade USA posters has grown to more than 64,000. Tony DiCicco, the new Women's National Team coach, Dorrance's former assistant, describes it as the best game he's ever witnessed—no unforced errors, high-quality—but most of us have to take his word for it. Because even though public interest in the team is surging,

→

U.S. goalkeeper Briana Scurry lunges to her left to punch away a penalty kick by China's Liu Yang in the dramatic shootout at the end of the 1999 World Cup final before 90,185 at the Rose Bowl—the largest crowd to ever watch a women's sporting event. "I knew all I had to do was stop one and we'd win it," said Scurry after the Americans triumphed in the shootout 5-4.

NBC does not broadcast most of the semifinals. They cut to the game only for overtime—for a handful of fraught, heightened minutes, just enough for the millions watching on TV to see Foudy tear through the midfield, slotting it to Shannon MacMillan, who sends the ball home in the 100th minute: The Americans down Norway 2-1 in sudden death overtime. As fathers across the country rage on about the imbeciles at NBC who show hours of platform diving but shortchange the most popular youth sport in the country, their twelve-year-old daughters sit quietly, chins in their hands, still thrilling. Those few minutes—the first time most kids have ever witnessed women's soccer—are enough to change everything. A generation of girls begins constructing a new dream: to play for the National Team one day.

NBC shows sporadic patches of the final versus China: Kristine Lilly flies up the left wing and knocks a cross into the box—Mia Hamm throws herself toward it, the China goalkeeper Gao dives and gets a hand on it and it bangs off the post—where MacMillan is waiting to slot it home. With the roar of 76,000 people ringing around Sanford Stadium in Athens, Georgia, MacMillan dives and slides across the grass, team dog-piling on top of her—the entire stadium jumping up and down. In the 31st minute, China equalizes. Now nearly the whole stadium is chanting U-S-A. Hamm threads a through-ball to Fawcett who sends it to Tiffany Milbrett—who beats the defender to score. The U.S. wins Olympic gold, and the minimal TV coverage makes the country hungry for more—they *want* women's soccer.

↓ Basking in the euphoria of their heart-stopping victory, the U.S. women's team celebrates the historic moment on the confetti-strewn Rose Bowl field with their World Cup trophy. Says U.S. President Bill Clinton, who is in attendance: "This is going to have a far-reaching impact not only in the United States but also in other countries."

ALL OF WHICH primes us for the mythical 1999 World Cup. Initially planned for small stadiums, the '96 Olympics makes everybody rethink things—U.S. Soccer president Alan Rothenberg and Maria Messing, head of the organizing committee, get the games moved to Giants Stadium, to the Rose Bowl. The players make sure that groundswell continues. While most celebrated athletes maintain a distance from their fans, the stars of the U.S. National Team—Overbeck, Foudy, Hamm, Lilly, Fawcett, Chastain—come to see you at your soccer camp. Huge crowds pack stadiums. Advertisers get on board: There are hip, funny commercials for Nike, for Adidas, for Gatorade. "Well, the revolution is here, and it has bright-red toenails,"*Sports Illustrated* columnist, Rick Reilly, wrote puckishly. "And it shops. And it carries diaper bags. The U.S. women's soccer team is towing the country around by the heart in this Women's World Cup, and just look at the players. They've got ponytails! They've got kids! They've got (gulp) curves!"

The country drinks them in: Here are players who love the game and love each other. They've been a close-knit group for over a decade, and when the media finally takes notice, the players still seem more attuned to each other than to the cameras. They are constantly playful, adopting a tongue-in-cheek attitude toward both gender expectations and fame. They call themselves "Booters with Hooters," send David Letterman a photo in which they're wearing nothing but *Late Night* T-shirts and their soccer cleats, and make an Austin Powers–themed spoof video mocking Chastain's naked photo shoot in *Gear* magazine, seemingly amused by the do-or-don't debate about cashing in on sex appeal. In Reilly's *Sports Illustrated* column, he relays an incident with Kate Sobrero (later Markgraf): When a guy at a bar asks her if she is gay, she delivers the wonderfully oblique and mischievous response: "No, but my girlfriend is." They are funny and genuine, smart and defiant: Watching them feels like glimpsing a group of friends you wish you could hang out with.

> **The country drinks them in. They've been a close-knit group for over a decade, . . . constantly playful, adopting a tongue-in-cheek attitude toward both gender expectations and fame.**

On the field, they put on a show; they deliver. They beat Denmark 3-0, Nigeria 7-1, North Korea 3-0. The quarterfinal game has high drama: Five minutes in, Chastain accidentally kicks the ball into her own goal. Overbeck gets face-to-face with Chastain and says, "Brandi. You are okay. We need you. You will win us this game." In the 49th minute, Brandi gets it back: Mia sends in a corner and Brandi scores a thumping header to equalize. They win 3-2.

They down Brazil 2-0 in the semis and then it's on to the final with 90,185 fans in the sold-out Rose Bowl. Forty million more watch on TV. It's ninety-five degrees. The starting eleven make a circle at midfield, put their heads together, and shout: Ooosa, oosa, oosa, ah!

For ninety minutes, it is tense, it is goal-less. Then comes overtime—golden goal, the first team to score wins. China's Fan Yunjie gets airborne and heads a rocket toward goal—past Scurry. Millions of Americans experience slow-motion horror: *China is going to score, we are going to lose.* But then eyes light upon a savior—Lilly is on the line! She leaps, she heads the ball. "Saved off the line!" the announcer shouts. "That ball was headed for goal!" But now the ball's in the six-yard box—loose among four Chinese players. A flying Chastain volleys the ball the hell out of there. In disbelief, fans all over the country are shouting and jumping and grasping each others' forearms: *Did that just happen?* Lilly, on the field, is asking herself the same question. That play says everything: They will not let themselves lose.

In the shootout, they are calm. They know they will win. Overbeck, Hamm, and Lilly run up to the penalty spot with total composure and score. U.S. goalkeeper Scurry almost never looks at China's shooters, but she does in the third round—and what she sees is fear. *This is the one.* She's bouncing on the line, as fierce and amped as she has ever felt in her life. She leaps left and punches the ball away. Then she roars, both fists pumping—90,000 erupting around her.

Finally, it's up to Chastain. She is the fifth shooter. If she scores, they win. She walks up and puts the ball on the spot. A breeze blows. She tucks her loose hair behind her ears, runs up—and buries it. What happens next becomes one of the most iconic images of the '90s: A euphoric Brandi rips off her jersey, face turned to the sky, mouth open, teammates rushing her, enveloping her, the whole stadium in a state of delirium.

In 2004, FIFA adds a law to the referee manual: "Removing one's shirt after scoring is unnecessary and players should avoid such excessive displays of joy." But on July 10, 1999, joy knows no bounds.

YEARS LATER, long after they've retired, Hamm, Foudy, and Cindy Parlow visit Overbeck in Chapel Hill. In a pack, they walk to the bus stop to pick up Carla's eighth grade son, Jackson. They wear U.S. jerseys that Carla has rounded up. As Jackson and his friends get off the bus, the USWNT alums say, "Y'all want to play some whiffle ball?"

They round up other neighborhood kids, some of whom are high school baseball players, and pit Jackson's friends against Mom's friends. Carla and Mia innocently inquire whether they should split up the teams to make it more even, but the high school baseball players scoff—it's even, they say.

Midgame, a high school kid hits the whiffle ball to Carla. She can't quite reach it with her hand so she pops it up with her foot, catches it with her right hand, tags the kid running from second to third, and then whips it to Mia, who's playing first base: double play.

One high school kid hollers, "You can't use your feet in whiffle ball!"

"It's whiffle ball—you can do whatever you want!" Foudy yells back.

Another high schooler—the one who just got tagged out—stares at Carla in wonder. "The moms I know can't do that," he says. Susan Ellis, a UNC soccer alum, says, "Well, are any of the moms you know gold medalists or World Cup champions?"

The moms, of course, win. As Parlow, Overbeck, Foudy, and Hamm walk away, they smile: It's a confident smile, the smile of women who are well-accustomed to victory, well-accustomed to inspiring future generations.

→ The U.S. Women would accept nothing less than victory. Here a jubilant Carla Overbeck hoists the 1999 World Cup trophy after their epoch-defining win over China.

> What happens next becomes one of the most iconic images of the '90s: A euphoric Brandi rips off her jersey. . . . On July 10, 1999, joy knows no bounds.

BY THE NUMBERS

49
Unanswered goals scored in five games against CONCACAF opponents en route to qualifying for the first Women's World Cup in 1991.

80
Minutes of regulation time in each game of the 1991 Women's World Cup in China. "They were afraid our ovaries were going to fall out, if we played the full ninety," said U.S. captain April Heinrichs.

1
Super Bowl played since the 1999 Women's World Cup final with a larger attendance than the 90,185 people who saw the U.S. defeat China in Pasadena. That 1999 WWC final had a higher attendance than fifty of the fifty-six Super Bowl games played through 2022.

2
U.S. media outlets who sent reporters to China to cover the 1991 World Cup: *USA Today* and *Soccer America.*

500+
Media outlets that covered the 1999 World Cup in the United States.

60K+
Fans from the original crowd of 73,123 at Stanford Stadium who attended the USWNT's 1999 World Cup semifinal win over Brazil and didn't stay for the men's part of the double-header between eventual MLS champion DC United and the hometown San Jose Earthquake.

OUTSIDE THE LINES

◀ **1991:** Madison Avenue takes notice of women's soccer as Umbro makes Michelle Akers the first female soccer player to get an endorsement deal from an equipment company. Soon after players like Mia Hamm (Nike), Kristine Lilly (Adidas), and Carla Overbeck (Fila) follow with deals of their own.

◀ **1994:** Joy Fawcett becomes the new face of a "soccer mom" by giving birth to her first child, Katelyn, and is soon featured in magazines like *Good Housekeeping, Shape,* and *Parents.*

◀ **1997:** *People* magazine includes Mia Hamm on its annual list of the "50 Most Beautiful People in the World."

1999: Hamm and her fellow North Carolina alumnus Michael Jordan appear in "Mia vs. Michael," a commercial for Gatorade set to the song "Anything You Can Do," that pits the superstars against each other in an array of athletic events ranging from basketball and soccer to fencing, judo, tennis, and running.

YEAR BY YEAR RESULTS

YEAR	1990	1991	1992	1993	1994	1995	1996
W-L-D	6-0-0	21-6-1	0-2-0	13-4-0	12-1-0	21-2-2	21-1-2
Tournament Wins	CAN, NA	W, C, ALB		C, I, COL	C, TRI, Q	U, F	O, B, U

ALG=Algarve Cup
ALB=Albena Cup
B=Brazil Cup
C=CONCACAF Women' Championship

CAN=Canada Cup
COL=Columbus Cup
F=Tournoi International Feminin
FN= Four Nations Tournament

G=CONCACAF Gold Cup
GG=Goodwill Games
I=CONCACAF Women's Invitational

NA=North America Cup
O=Olympics
PQ=Peace Queen Cup
Q=Chiquita Cup
S=SheBelieves Cup

MILESTONES

100TH CAP

AUG. 6, 1995 KRISTINE LILLY
First American, male or female, to reach 100 caps (or international matches played)

JAN. 16, 1996	**MIA HAMM**
JAN. 20, 1996	**CARIN JENNINGS-GABARRA**
MAY 12, 1996	**MICHELLE AKERS**
JULY. 23, 1996	**JOY FAWCETT**
AUG. 1, 1996	**CARLA OVERBECK**
APR. 24, 1997	**JULIE FOUDY**
MAY 10, 1998	**TISHA VENTURINI**
SEPT. 18, 1998	**TIFFENY MILBRETT**

100TH GOAL

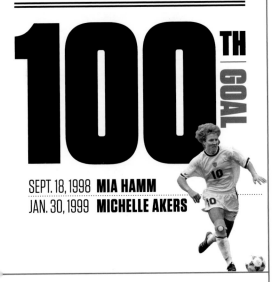

SEPT. 18, 1998 MIA HAMM
JAN. 30, 1999 MICHELLE AKERS

1997	1998	1999
16-2-0	22-1-2	25-2-2
U	U, GG, FN	W, U

T=Tournament of Nations
TRI=Tri-Nations Tournament
U=U.S. Women's Cup
W=Women's World Cup

DECADE LEADERS 1990–1999

CAPS		GOALS		WINS	
KRISTINE LILLY	178	**MIA HAMM**	114	**BRIANA SCURRY**	83
MIA HAMM	168	**MICHELLE AKERS**	101	**MARY HARVEY**	20
JULIE FOUDY	166	**KRISTINE LILLY**	79	**SASKIA WEBBER**	19
CARLA OVERBECK	153	**TIFFENY MILBRETT**	68	**TRACY DUCAR**	14
JOY FAWCETT	140	**CARIN GABARRA**	48		

THE ALL-DECADE XI

MIA **HAMM**   MICHELLE **AKERS**   TIFFENY **MILBRETT**

KRISTINE **LILLY**   JULIE **FOUDY**   TISHA **VENTURINI**

BRANDI **CHASTAIN**   KATE **MARKGRAF**   CARLA **OVERBECK**   JOY **FAWCETT**

BRIANA **SCURRY**

Selected by a panel of current and former USWNT players, coaches, and members of the media. See page 254.

Brandi Chastain, the player her teammates call "Hollywood," lives up to the billing and fashions a blockbuster ending with her decisive penalty kick to win the 1999 World Cup.

A hell-bent Carin Jennings winner of the Golden Ball awarded to the best player at the 1991 World Cup, makes a typically slashing run against Norway in the victorious title match.

"I think it was the start of the U.S. Women's National Team program that won three World Cups and four Olympic medals," Carin Jennings says of 1991. "That culture of competitive mentality and hard work, along with talent, has never wavered. Every person who has ever played for the U.S. National Team is connected in that regard."

KIERAN THEIVAM & JEFF KASSOUF,
The Making of the Women's World Cup

Foudy's first National Team coach, Anson Dorrance, predicted that someday we would be calling her Senator Foudy. Sporting an infectious smile, a cutting wit, sharp debating skills, and an intellect that challenged interviewers to be at their best, she could spar with them all. When Dorrance, an accomplished debater himself, teased her about choosing Stanford over his University of North Carolina, he told her she passed up four national championships. She quickly fired back, "I chose an education instead."

↑ Julie Foudy helps kick off the Americans' triumphant 1999 World Cup run with a goal in the opening game against Denmark at Giants Stadium in East Rutherford, New Jersey.

GEMMA CLARKE, *Soccer Women*

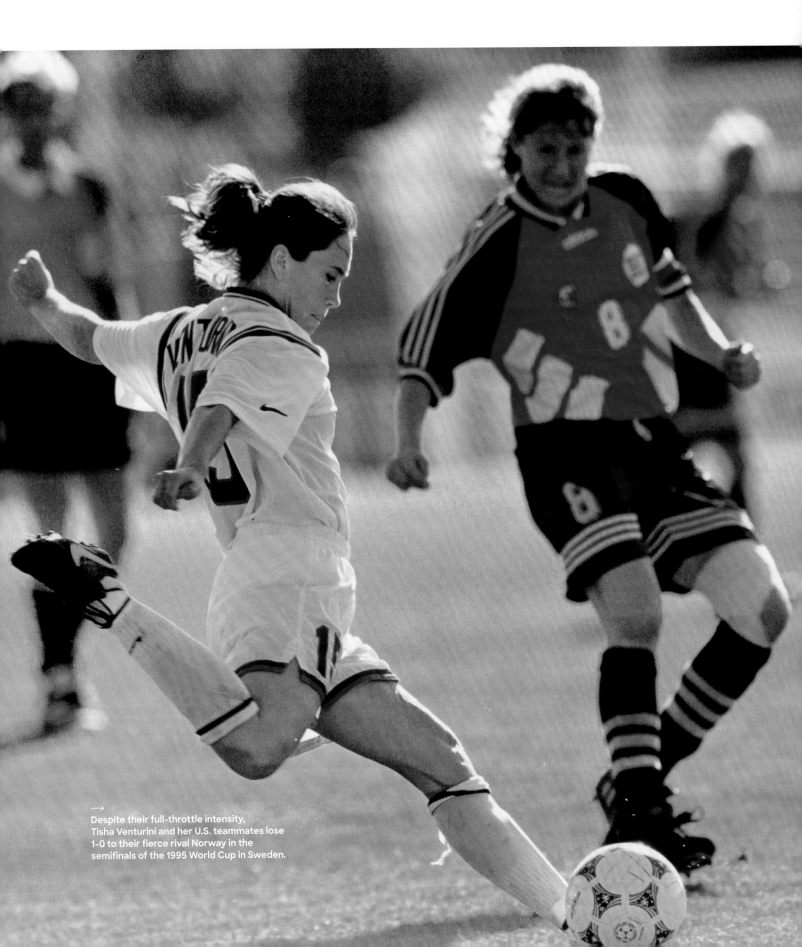

Despite their full-throttle intensity, Tisha Venturini and her U.S. teammates lose 1-0 to their fierce rival Norway in the semifinals of the 1995 World Cup in Sweden.

The women on the American soccer team . . . were pioneers, they made their own tradition. They began the team in anonymity, and, now, they had not only to play the game, but they had to build the World Cup's public awareness and to secure its financial viability. If they failed, not only the team, but the World Cup and the professional viability of the sport, might fail. This responsibility, this stepping onto a ledge of chance and venture and precarious gamble brought great pressure, but it also invested the American women with a vigorous sense of purpose, trust, reliance, and competitive resolve.

JERÉ LONGMAN, *The Girls of Summer*

→
Two of the standouts in the U.S. women's first World Cup championship in 1991 were captain April Heinrichs (left) who scored four times in the tournament, and Shannon Higgins, who assisted on both goals in the 2-1 victory over Norway in the final.

When the U.S. players took their flight to the 1991 World Cup in China, they were confused as to why they were flying the opposite way around the world. In an apparent money-saving move, the plane from the U.S. stopped to pick up the Swedish and Norwegian teams along the way.

"Then when we went home, instead of just crossing the Pacific Ocean, we went all the way back around to drop everybody off and then landed in New York," remembers Brandi Chastain, who first became a National Team regular in 1986.

Shannon Higgins, a member of the USWNT from 1987-1991, says the players didn't have their own uniforms for years—they wore hand-me-downs from the Men's National Team that didn't fit. The 1991 World Cup was the first time that the women wore kits designed especially for them.

CAITLIN MURRAY, *The National Team*

→ For two decades, women's soccer looked to Mia Hamm to be its savior and she didn't disappoint, scoring 158 international goals before she retired in 2004.

Does the face launch the movement? Or does the movement launch the face? At some point the two entwine, and no one can say. At some point little girls begin roaming the team's hotel hallways, looking for Mia, and after she poses for a picture and begins to walk away, they say, our whole team's waiting outside for you, can you come? At some point they begin falling asleep with her face on their walls and ceilings, the last image on their retinas each day, this woman who convinces them, without uttering a word, that it's OK to sweat, seethe, leap, let go. They begin writing her letters, wearing her ponytail and number 9 jersey to her games and shrieking, "Mia! Mia!" at the same pitch and frenzy as starving baby birds.

GARY SMITH,
Sports Illustrated

→
In the first minute of the first youth game in which he saw her play, Anson Dorrance picked out Mia Hamm and knew he was witnessing a generational talent.

"I remember having a meeting with the team," [Anson] Dorrance said. "I asked them a rhetorical question. I told them there are two ways to go into this World Cup: One is to sneak in on cat's paws and surprise everyone; the other way is to go in with your flag flying, trumpets blaring, and say, 'We are the best.' I was not a cat's paw kind of guy. I wanted to go in and say, 'Here we are. Give us your best shot.' It was a wonderfully powerful mentality that we went in with."

TIM NASH, *It's Not the Glory*

43

Wendy Gebauer, one of the University of North Carolina players who formed the core of the 1991 USWNT, skips past a Japanese defender en route to scoring a goal as the Americans go on to win their first World Cup title.

France's Davis Cup victory over the U.S. was certainly unusual: It last happened in 1932. But America's disappointment in tennis was softened by an even greater surprise in soccer: an upset win by the U.S. team in the first women's World Cup.

This was the first world championship for an American soccer squad of either sex. It was especially delicious because the U.S. will play host to the next men's championship, in 1994, even as it struggles for respect in the world's most popular sport. The men's squad, with a new coach, has improved remarkably since losing in the first round of the 1990 World Cup. But it won't easily match what the women pulled off in China, edging favored Norway in the final minutes of the final game.

While some countries have professional women's teams, America's is anything but. Coach Anson Dorrance also coaches the women's program at the University of North Carolina. Two women on his national squad are college coaches, another quit school to train for the championship and still another is a Stanford pre-med student who got her midterm exam in China by fax.

Their spirit and skill made history last Saturday. The roster of women's World Cup winners will forever list America first.

OP-ED PAGE, *The New York Times*

↓ In full beast mode, Michelle Akers powers a header against Norway at the 1996 Olympics in Athens, Georgia. The U.S. wins their semifinal showdown 2–1.

"We hated Norway. We always hated them," says Akers. "They were good, they were tough, they were bitchy, they talked smack. I hated them, but it was fun. I loved hating them. It was great. For me, the more I hate them the harder I end up playing."

—

ALEX ABNOS, *"Start of Something Big," SI.com*

Few players embodied the fierce winning mindset of the U.S. more than April Heinrichs, the team captain and future coach. Here she leads the Americans to their 1991 World Cup title in China.

From their confident strut and their cool sunglasses, you wouldn't think that this group of women is about to play the most important game of their lives—and perhaps the most important in the history of women's soccer—in just a few days. Their victory over China in the 1999 World Cup final would ignite an explosion of excitement that fueled the sport's popularity around the globe.

"We didn't play for the recognition," Heinrichs said. "We didn't play for the money. We played for the opportunity to put ourselves against the best in the world and hopefully to one day call ourselves the best in the world. That's what motivated me. Waking up thinking, 'OK, if there's someone out there working harder than me, I better work harder. If there's a team out there better than us, we need to work harder. If all of us improve by 1 per cent, we'll get better."

KIERAN THEIVAM & JEFF KASSOUF,
The Making of the Women's World Cup

In athletes, we recognize women who own their bodies, inhabiting every inch of them, and the sight of their vitality is exhilarating. Our own potential has become apparent, thanks to their example. We want to be like them—alive all over.

HOLLY BRUBACH, *New York Times Magazine*

"It's okay to get after someone for doing something wrong," Overbeck said,"but when they do something right, you have to let them know too."

TIM NASH, *It's Not the Glory*

←
Carla Overbeck leaps in celebration after scoring the first penalty kick in the championship shootout against China in 1999. The U.S. captain's confidence and composure inspired her teammates to follow her lead.

...If you asked a hundred people who the captain of the team was, odds are none of them would name Carla Overbeck. It's unlikely they would even remember her name—in large part because that's the way she wanted it.... At five foot seven, Overbeck isn't especially tall or muscular. Growing up in the Dallas suburbs, she was such a twig—with skinny legs and arms—that her dad used to call her termite. On the field, she wore her long brown hair in a tight ponytail, and though she was famous among her teammates for her salty language, her face was so cold and stony that she rarely betrayed emotions.... She was a defender whose skills, according to one former coach, were "average at best." She did not project the kind of confidence, or game-changing ability, leaders are supposed to display.

But Overbeck's humility had an upside for the team. By getting rid of the ball as soon as she had the opportunity, she increased the amount of time it was at the feet of superior athletes—and because she rarely left the pitch, this selfless instinct helped the team generate more scoring chances. The same functional mentality touched everything she did, even off the field. When the U.S. team arrived at a hotel after some grueling international flight, Overbeck would carry everyone's bags to their hotel rooms. "I'm the captain," she explained, "but I'm no better than anybody else. I'm certainly not a better soccer player."

SAM WALKER, *The Captain Class*

←
Out of substitutes after starting goalkeeper Briana Scurry is red carded in the dying minutes against Denmark in the 1995 World Cup, Mia Hamm is called upon to pull on the gloves and preserve the win.

My international goalkeeping debut was to face a free kick about as close to the goal as could be from a woman who would like nothing better than to blast me halfway across the Atlantic. I really don't remember what I was thinking at the time but looking back, I realize I wasn't well positioned. I was too far behind the wall instead of shaded toward the open part of the net (that's goalkeeper talk, thank you). Well, wouldn't you know it? The shooter took a big run up and sent the ball sailing over the crossbar. I like to think I would have saved it anyway, but, of course, we'll never know.

MIA HAMM, *Go for the Goal: A Champion's Guide to Winning in Soccer and Life*

They were a rare combination—jock sex symbols with a social conscience, best friends who turned into lethal competitors once the games began. They probed a long and often difficult ninety-minute match for the pivot point when they could feel their opponent's resolve breaking, and their mentality became, "Jump right on them, finish them off, try to bury them," as [Kristine] Lilly once said.

"It was not accepted to be a female athlete at all," says [U.S. forward] Carin Jennings "And every day I'd go to school, someone would ask me about sports, and I'd say, 'Oh, I don't play sports.' I denied it all the way through high school, because it wasn't the cool thing to do."

JOHNETTE HOWARD, *ESPN.com*

Kristine Lilly, the all-time leader in caps (men or women), scores a goal against Denmark in the opening game of the 1999 World Cup in front of a sold-out crowd at Giants Stadium.

←
The most experienced and underrated player in the world, Kristine Lilly, is among the other U.S. stars who go unnoticed by the American TV audience, thanks to a network blackout of the Olympic final in 1996.

> ## "I showed the team a picture of Michelle one day," coach Anson Dorrance said, "and on her face was written her mentality—almost a competitive anger. It was a visual still of fury."

JERÉ LONGMAN, *New York Times*

Memo to NBC: In case you missed it—and, certainly, millions of American TV viewers have—a nifty little Olympic soccer tournament comes to a close tonight at Sanford Stadium in Athens, Ga.

Memo II to NBC: Almost forgot—the Americans will play for the gold medal.

Memo III: American women!

While NBC's cameras have been following every hop, skip, and Yurchenko performed on the women's gymnastic podium . . . the U.S. women's soccer team has labored beneath the radar, despite a roster full of engaging personalities, a 3-0-1 record, a scintillating semifinal overtime victory over Norway, and a real chance to win the first U.S. gold medal in Olympic soccer.

MIKE PENNER, *Los Angeles Times*

The indomitable Michelle Akers, seen here against Norway in the 1996 Olympics, comes out on top in another aerial battle.

→
Waving the flag in Olympic triumph, Joy Fawcett, Carin Jennings and Cindy Parlow (following behind Fawcett) take a victory lap after beating China for the gold.

←
Joy Fawcett's one-year-old daughter, Katelyn, takes the field at the 1995 Women's World Cup, cheered on by her mom, Mia Hamm, and Kristine Lilly.

Joy Fawcett stood transfixed under the stands of a college football field turned Olympic football field. She had a gold medal around her neck and her two-year-old daughter, Katelyn, in her arms. It had been ninety minutes since the U.S. had edged China 2-1 in the first Olympic women's soccer final, in which Fawcett had made a brilliant run from her right-back position to help create the winning goal. But she considered the U.S. triumph less a win for herself or for her team than a victory for her extended family: the 76,481 spectators who had filled Sanford Stadium in Athens, Ga., last Thursday, the little girl named Lindsay who had sent U.S. players homemade red-white-and-blue twill anklets and bracelets, and every schoolgirl who had written to say, "Sorry I'm bugging you, but I think you're the greatest."

This victory was also for Katelyn. "I hope she can do the same thing," said Joy, twenty eight. "I hope she has more opportunities and finds it a lot easier than I did. If she chooses this sport and gets to this level, there should be much more recognition."

MICHAEL FARBER, *Sports Illustrated*

For three mind-boggling weeks, they were everywhere you looked—the Mini Mias, the Rowdy Foudys, the Fawcett Fanatics—ponytails held in place by little soccer balls, sleeves rolled up around their shoulders just like their role models, faces luminous with dreams they never dreamed before. They are what will endure about this World Cup long after the huge crowds and media jackals have moved on to the next Big Event. . . . In the battle for the hearts and minds of everyone's favorite demo—Teen USA—the American women not only beat back the Chinese, the Brazilians, and the Germans, but also obliterated 'N Sync, Buffy, Dawson, and the rest of the Hollywood-created pop icons who formerly claimed the devotion of the *Tiger Beat* crowd.

DAVID HIRSHEY,
ESPN The Magazine

The most significant goal in Brandi Chastain's career is not the one you're thinking about. Not the left-footed penalty kick at the sold-out Rose Bowl that decided the final of the 1999 Women's World Cup.

Chastain's most important goal is one that's known as either "the redemption goal" or her "second goal" against Germany in the 1999 World Cup quarterfinal. The "first goal" Chastain scored in that game happened to be an own goal in the 5th minute putting the U.S. in an early hole.

Germany is certainly not the type of team you'd want to spot an early goal, but that's what happened when Chastain and goalkeeper Briana Scurry failed to communicate. With Scurry running off her line, Chastain played what she thought to be an innocuous back pass to her keeper.

As soon as the ball left Chastain's right foot, she sensed the error, taking a few hard steps to try and chase the ball, only to realize it was too late.

Midfielder Julie Foudy says the message to Chastain was clear. "Our captain Carla Overbeck told her right away. We need you to just keep playing. We've got this."

Just four minutes after the interval the U.S. had a corner kick. The ball was played to the back post where a German defender inadvertently headed the ball into the center of the box about eight yards out. Chastain, who had made a run to the near post, peeled back toward the center of the box and was able to catch the ball perfectly on the short hop with the inside of her right foot, falling to her knee after contact. The ball caromed off the inside of the right post and over the line, tying the score in a game the U S. went on to win 3-2.

"I'm really proud of that goal minus the circumstances," Chastain says. "So many coaches taught me to do things the right way under pressure. So that was a good moment for me to say that in the big game, at an important time, the technique came through. As a player that's cool."

JEFF BRADLEY, *SI.com*

← After inadvertently putting the ball into her own net earlier, Brandi Chastain's face is etched with elation and relief following her game-tying goal against Germany in the 1999 World Cup quarterfinals.

The acrobatic goalkeeping of Briana Scurry keeps Brazil at bay in this 1999 World Cup semifinal won by the U.S. 2–0. It becomes Scurry's third clean sheet in five World Cup matches and her fifty-second career shutout in ninety-five international appearances.

"Briana Scurry at her peak—no one has ever played better than that for the USA," said Tony DiCicco, who coached Scurry for five years on the Women's National Team. "She was the best in the world."

CAITLIN DEWEY, *Washington Post*

If she misses the kick that decides this World Cup, she'll have to live inside those flames until her final breath . . . . She is chosen to kick fourth for the Americans. They're up 3-2—the third Chinese attempt was punched away by U.S. goalkeeper Briana Scurry—when Mia approaches the white dot. If she scores, the Chinese are against the wall. She places the ball on the dot, pushes a strand of hair from her face. She will remember nothing from then until the ball strikes the net, and the Rose Bowl explodes. She screams, but her face never relaxes, never smiles, her eyes still burning and her jaw clenched as she races back to her teammates. She is not a woman celebrating. She's a woman howling I beat you, goddammit, at all her fear and doubt.

GARY SMITH, *Sports Illustrated*

↑ Shannon MacMillan comes off the bench to become an unexpected hero of the 1996 U.S Olympic team, scoring three goals, including this overtime winner against Norway in the semifinal.

← One of the most lethal finishers in USWNT history, Tiffeny Milbrett led the Americans in scoring in the 1999 World Cup, including this goal against Nigeria.

One is fast and the other is quick and both have exceptional soccer skills. They also are exceptions to the stereotype that any premier female player in this country must be a suburban princess from a sitcom-perfect home.

Shannon MacMillan and Tiffeny Milbrett are partners in crime, arsonists who can light up a game in an instant. They were a tandem at the University of Portland, where they were known as the M&M line, and spent two seasons with the same Japanese pro club.

They scored a combined five goals for the 1996 Olympic gold-medal team, divvying up the most important ones. MacMillan struck in sudden death against Norway in the semifinal; Milbrett pounded in the medal-clincher against China.

BONNIE DESIMONE, *Chicago Tribune*

An overflowing Rose Bowl crowd along with an American TV audience of 40 million watch the U.S. and China play a game for the ages in the 1999 World Cup final.

TODAY'S RECORD ATTENDANCE IS 90,185

WOMEN'S

25:32

HYUNDAI   McDonald's

"Coming out on the field, I kept thinking that for so long we had talked about how successful this team is and what a draw it could be," Foudy said. "Every time someone comes to watch, they fall in love with this team. And then I thought of all the negatives we heard. Five months before the World Cup, we had a press conference to announce the draw. The first two questions, we get hammered by Americans. 'You're lying about ticket sales. You haven't sold as many as you say you have. You're downsizing the stadiums and you won't admit it. You're crazy to do this.' That was the theme of it. I was like, man, that's always the attitude. 'You shouldn't, you can't, it's not going to happen.' And then I walked into this huge stadium and I kind of looked around and smiled and said, 'Yes.' I knew some attitudes had changed."

JERÉ LONGMAN, *The Girls of Summer*

→
Kate Sobrero didn't lose too many
duels in a twelve-year career that saw
her make 201 appearances for the
National Team and go on to become
the USWNT's general manager.

At twenty two, the youngest of the American defenders,
Sobrero [later Markgraf] was funny, spacy–brilliant, a dean's
list graduate in business-science from Notre Dame who
wore a tongue stud and her hair dyed red from a lost bet with
a teammate. She spoke on permanent fast-forward and had
overcome bizarre injury and dispirited confidence to become
a reliable, sturdy presence. Unlike Overbeck, who rushed
in to poke the ball away, Sobrero relied on her speed and agility
and what soccer players called "hardness," a gritty willingness
for the interior scrap, the shoulder-ram and arm-slap and
elbow-jostle of marking a forward, teeth biting her lower lip,
a competitive fearlessness from having played with three
brothers, a patient physical insistence that eventually forced
her opponent to make a mistake, to turn the wrong way or
to kick the ball too far to be retrieved. A self-described tomboy,
she said she had been angry to learn as a girl that she would
not be allowed to play competitive football.

JERÉ LONGMAN, *The Girls of Summer*

For almost the entire game the Americans had harried China with their version of a full-court press—the 100 defense—which prevented the Chinese midfielders from giving quick support to their forwards. But with [Michelle] Akers off the field during extra time, the Chinese began attacking with greater abandon. After taking just two shots on goal in the game's regulation ninety minutes, they fired three in the thirty-minute extra time, including one that should have been decisive: defender Fan Yunjie's header off a corner kick. "I was like, Uh-oh, the ball's behind me," Scurry said later. But so, too, was Lilly. Stationed at her usual spot on the near post, she headed the ball off the goal line. "Just doing my job," Lilly said.

GRANT WAHL, *Sports Illustrated*

←
"One time in a hundred that she had to be there, and she was," said USWNT coach Tony DiCicco of Lilly's World Cup-saving header off the line.

With her almost supernatural acceleration, Mia Hamm was a force of nature on the field. Here, in a "friendly" against Mexico prior to the '99 World Cup, she looks anything but neighborly as she leaves a hapless defender in her wake.

Let's remember [Hamm] as the bridge, the one all the ponytailed phenoms are climbing across to leave behind the 20th century, when so many women had to feel apologetic about going for it all, in order to reach the 21st, when they'll all be standing on the white dot waiting for the ball, and the photo op, and the commercial.

——

GARY SMITH, *Sports Illustrated*

When I was playing, they said soccer was a man's world and that women should remain on the sidelines. All I can say is, I'm glad I never had to go up against Mia Hamm.

——

PELÉ

As Chastain's penalty kick bulges the net, her ecstatic teammates run to swarm her. Mia Hamm (third from right), overcome with emotion, tearfully keeps repeating, "Are you kidding me? Are you kidding me?"

→

In the 1999 World Cup final, Brandi Chastain's delirious, muscle-flexing, jersey-doffing celebration would come to define the rise of women's sports in America.

Who could have guessed that America's proudest moment this summer would come when 90,000 people watched a woman take her shirt off? "Momentary insanity," U.S. defender Brandi Chastain explained. But no explanation was necessary. Her team had just won the Women's World Cup, ending three weeks of insanity. Chastain converted the final shootout kick of the tournament Saturday for a one-goal victory over China, then pulled off her jersey, just as many men do after they score. Her gesture wasn't very revealing; she was wearing a sports bra.... But no matter. She was the picture of competitiveness, of everything people used to believe women couldn't be.

GWEN KNAPP, *San Francisco Examiner*

2001

OTHER COUNTRIES SOUGHT TO MATCH THE U.S. WOMEN'S SKILL AND ATHLETICISM BUT THEY LACKED ONE CRUCIAL ELEMENT: AMERICA'S WINNING MENTALITY, AS PERSONIFIED BY THE POWER AND RESOLVE OF ABBY WAMBACH, WHO MADE SURE THE FIGHTING SPIRIT RAGED ON.

Starting in 2001, the USWNT's Abby Wambach began tearing apart defenses and didn't stop until she had scored 184 goals, the most of any man or woman in U.S. Soccer history.

→ Brazil's Formiga has nowhere to turn as Kristine Lilly and Shannon Boxx hound her in the 2004 Olympic gold medal game in Athens, Greece.

NEVER DEFEND ALONE

BY GWENDOLYN OXENHAM

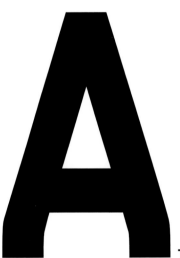

AT THE 2002 National Team camp, seventeen-year-old rookie Heather O'Reilly sleeps through her alarm and misses team breakfast. Flustered, she throws on her gear and makes it to training on time—*No one noticed,* she tells herself. *I'm in the clear.*

O'Reilly's relief is premature: The next training session, captain Julie Foudy calls the team together. "It's come to my attention that some of us have been missing meals, showing up late to things," says Foudy. "That's not what this team is about. As a group we need to pay the price for these mistakes: We're going to do full-field sprints."

O'Reilly, in the back of the group, panics: *Oh my god, this is terrible. This is my fault.* But also—fitness is her bread and butter. *I better crush these,* she thinks. *Or else I'm never getting invited back.* She gets on the end line and when the coach drops her hand, O'Reilly takes off, flying. She looks to her left, looks to her right, doesn't see anybody. "And I had the audacity to think that it was because I was so far in front of these women, these world-class athletes," O'Reilly says with a laugh. She gets about fifty yards out before she realizes everybody else stopped a few steps in, keeled over with laughter, watching how far this kid would run on her own. "It was a prank, to kind of put their arm around me and be like, Yeah, we know you missed breakfast—don't do it again." This is their way of inducting her into the culture of the team, as if to say: We laugh and tease and enjoy each other—but also, we don't miss breakfast, we don't take shortcuts. Everything counts.

MORE THAN ANYTHING ELSE, that's what this opening decade of the twenty-first century is about: passing down the ways of the team. A changing of the guard is coming: Mia, Julie, Brandi, Joy, and Carla are on the way out, and they want the team ethos to live beyond them. Coach Anson Dorrance had sought out and encouraged players who were unapologetically confident, ready to take on anyone and eschew convention in favor of instinct. He called it the "USA mentality."

That creative self-belief was fired in what Dorrance had referred to as a "competitive cauldron"—every drill in every practice was a fight to be won, all results recorded and posted. That cauldron fostered tough players who craved wins and turned loss into fuel. Tony DiCicco, Anson Dorrance's former assistant and successor as head coach for the 1995 and 1999 World Cups, carried forward this environment of hunger and passion. Exuding infectious enthusiasm, DiCicco frequently took the field with his arms spread wide, announcing, "I love my job!" That too is part of what it means to play with this team: You not only compete, you *enjoy* competing. But in the 2000s, that joyful vigor would become severely tested.

First, the 2000 Sydney Olympics: With fabled trailblazer April Heinrichs as the new head coach, the Americans head to Australia with their usual self-assurance. But when they hit the 90th minute of the gold medal game, the score line is Norway 2, United States 1: The almighty Americans are about to lose. In the dying seconds of the game, Hamm drives a perfect cross to Tiffeny Milbrett. And Milbrett, who is barely five-foot-two,

A changing of the guard is coming: Mia, Julie, Brandi, Joy, and Carla are on the way out, and they want the team ethos to live beyond them.

→
An unexpected starter and an even more surprising star, Angela Hucles becomes the second-leading goal scorer at the 2008 Beijing Olympics.

←
Tiffeny Milbrett (16) joyously slides to celebrate the first of her two goals in the 2000 Olympic final loss to Norway.

rises over the Norwegian captain Linda Medalen and heads the ball home: The Americans never-say-die, every-second-counts mentality is once again on rampant display.

On the sideline, the Norwegian coach Per-Mathias Høgmo, sinks to his knees. Norwegian defender Gro Espeseth recalls thinking with exasperation, *Do they always have to win?*

The answer, it turns out, is no. The Americans lose that game in sudden-death overtime. The losing does not end there. They return from their Olympic disappointment to launch the first women's professional soccer league in the United States, the Women's United Soccer Association (WUSA): This league is their baby, the dream they've fought for so that women would have the chance to make a living playing the game. For players like Angela Hucles and Shannon Boxx, this league changes everything. Hucles, a star at UVA, had taken a job at a plumbing company after graduation; Boxx, a star at Notre Dame, had been headed to graduate school. But WUSA gives them an opening: Hucles, a few years out of college and pretty much off the radar, now has a stage on which to perform. The ninety-third player picked in the 2000 WUSA draft, she plays her way onto the National Team. Boxx, playing for the San Diego Spirit, alongside the likes of Julie Foudy and Joy Fawcett, does the same; she becomes the first American woman to score three goals in her first three matches with the National Team.

But on September 15, 2003, days before the opening of the World Cup, just three years after it began, WUSA announces the league is folding.

This loss is the hardest. The veterans—the players who fought to create this league—feel it on so many levels: They think about their professional club teammates, who no longer have a place to play. They think about the undiscovered Angela Hucleses and Shannon Boxxes— the players who will graduate from college and hang up the cleats without ever getting a chance to see how good they could be. And they think about the kids they've coached at camps and chatted with after games, who will wake up to the news that the dream of "becoming a professional soccer player" is no longer possible.

Five days after the league folds, the U.S. National Team—reigning champions—heads into the 2003 World Cup. The demise of the league casts a shadow over the tournament. Still, they intend to play break-your-heart beautiful soccer—to say, *Here is what will disappear.*

Among the new faces is Cat Reddick (later Whitehill), a defender with a soft Alabama drawl who studies for finals at UNC while playing in the World Cup, where she scores twice in her first game. There are Santa Clara alums Danielle Slaton, an attack-minded defender, and Aly Wagner, a crafty midfielder, savvy on the ball. And there's twenty-three-year-old Abby Wambach, a five-foot-eleven force of nature and aerial wonder. From Rochester, New York, she is the youngest of seven kids—"Soccer," she says, "was my way to be heard." She had spent the previous two years playing beside Mia Hamm for the Washington Freedom, soaking up as much as she could. In the World Cup quarterfinals, when the U.S. is facing its Norwegian nemesis, Reddick drives the ball into Wambach, who pivots and soars, flicking the ball into the goal for the

A Wambach header—an act of power and grace—will become a defining feature of the American style of play for the next fifteen years.

↓ Playing the opening match of the 2003 World Cup in Washington DC's RFK Stadium, Shannon Boxx puts a header out of reach of the goalkeeper and the game out of reach for Sweden.

win. A Wambach header—an act of power and grace—would become a defining feature of the American style of play for the next fifteen years.

But in the semifinal, it's Germany who rises to the occasion. The Americans are dethroned emphatically, 3-0.

IN APRIL 2004, April Heinrichs calls thirty players into a six-month residency camp in Los Angeles to prepare for the upcoming Olympics in Greece, though only eighteen players will make the final roster. They rent apartments and houses across the South Bay. The veterans (who refer to themselves as "the Old Bags") rent a house in Manhattan Beach; the younger generation share apartments scattered nearby.

Four of the kids still in college have side-by-side apartments in nearby Hermosa Beach: Heather O'Reilly rooms with UNC teammate Lori Chalupny, a St. Louis native whom Anson Dorrance describes as one of his "top three players of all time"—complete and unrelenting. Next door are best friends Lindsay Tarpley and Leslie Osborne, who have played together on the Midwestern regional team since they were eleven years old. Tarpley, a forward as soft-spoken and hardworking as Hamm, gets a bag of balls after each training session and practices long-range shots. Osborne, a defender, is as extroverted and social as Tarpley is shy. None of them has any idea what their chances are of making the team.

↑ Outshooting their opponent 23-0, Aly Wagner and the USWNT are on a different plane than Chinese Taipei, handing out a 10-0 drubbing in a World Cup qualifying warm-up.

The camp, which multiple players describe as "the toughest of all time," is fitness-heavy. The session after lunch is the most dreaded: It's 800s—a half mile on the grass, lap after lap run at a near-sprint. Beyond the communion of shared exhaustion, they spend their downtime together: Several acquire beach cruisers and develop a ritual of riding to coffee shops; Wambach and O'Reilly play in pickup volleyball games on the beach. The veterans host brunches on off days. For six months, the kids learn from the core 99ers—from "Loudy Foudy" and Brandi "Hollywood" Chastain, vocal leaders who shout encouragement, to the quieter vets, like Hamm, Fawcett, and Lilly—who check on their progress. "Because they each led so differently, there was something for everyone," notes Tarpley. "Always, they made you feel heard. They cared what we had to say. And they were so

positive, so determined—they helped you find those qualities in yourself."

The last day of camp Heinrichs posts a list in the locker room. O'Reilly has landed what she knows must be one of the final tickets to Greece. Tarpley, also, is on the list. Their roommates, Chalupny and Osborne, who are standing right beside them, are not. This too is part of the National Team cauldron—every single tournament, talented players fight for an extremely limited number of spots on the roster.

CRETE, GREECE—2004 Summer Games. In the crystal-clear waters of the Mediterranean, on their off day from Olympic training, the players float on inflatable rafts, holding on to each other's ankles, one connected chain—taking a moment to soak in where they are and what they want: a gold medal.

At residency camp, they'd developed a motto, a strategy: Never defend alone. Send two defenders for every attacker; have each others' backs. This philosophy matters most in the final against Brazil: The Brazilians are ball-sorcerers, individually magnificent. The American defenders, in sync and attuned to one another, endure opening waves of the Brazilian attack.

Tarpley, who acts as a super-sub in the group games, becomes the starting attacking center mid. The twenty-year-old has spent months living shoulder-to-shoulder with her heroes—often, quite literally. Days earlier, to her horror, she'd spilled red Gatorade across the white carpet of their Greek hotel room, and Hamm, her roommate, had gotten down on her knees alongside Tarpley and helped her scrub. She has savored each small exchange with the 99ers. Like the game in Portugal, when Tarpley played a safe ball and Foudy had instructed her to go for the jugular: "Tarp! Why do you keep doing that? Play the dangerous ball! I know you can do it!" And Tarp thought, *You're right, I can.* Now she is ready to prove it.

In the 39th minute, Tarpley runs at the Brazilian defenders and they keep dropping—so she cracks a shot from twenty yards out. All those postpractice shot sessions pay off: The ball sails into the goal and puts the US up 1-0. In the 112th minute, Lilly sends in a corner. Wambach, ten yards out, launches herself skyward and does what she does best: heads the ball home. Tarpley and Wambach, the next generation of stars, give a parting gift to the 99ers, who have imbued them with the never-defend-alone, have-each-other's-back mentality. The passing of the baton is complete.

↑ Still a month shy of her twenty-first birthday, Lindsay Tarpley moves past a Brazilian challenge to score the most important goal of her life which gives the U.S. an early edge in the 2004 gold medal game.

← Knowing she'll go out as a champion, longtime USWNT captain Julie Foudy celebrates with Wambach (16), the hero of the 2004 Olympics.

THE 2007 WORLD CUP is the first major tournament without the 99 legends. The US is seeking World Cup redemption. What they get is World Cup embarrassment: They suffer their worst defeat ever, losing 4-0 in the semifinals to Brazil. The Brazilians' fourth goal is perhaps the most spectacular ever scored in a women's World Cup: Marta does a juggling back-heel around one U.S. defender, cuts by another, and slots it past one more—"a circus act" as the *New York Times* described it. In comparison, the U.S. looks pedestrian.

Hope Solo, a young, fierce goalkeeper who starts every other game that tournament, watches from the bench. U.S. coach Greg Ryan, Heinrichs's former assistant, starts Briana Scurry instead, based on her stellar past performances against the Brazilians. After the game, Solo tells reporters that Ryan made the wrong decision—that she would have made those saves. That dissent is very different than the tight-unit vibe to which the public is accustomed; this is *not* having each others' backs. The U.S. team has reached its nadir.

Who better to lift them up than former Swedish star Pia Sundhage, who waltzes into her first team meeting as National Team coach in 2008 strumming a guitar and singing Bob Dylan's "The Times They Are A-Changin'." In recent years, it felt like U.S. goals never seemed to come from the run of play, only from set pieces, the team employing a "dreary direct style," as *The Guardian* put it. Sundhage is going to change that: "She brought us calm, confidence," says veteran defender Kate Markgraf. "She wanted us to play beautiful, possession-orientated soccer." Sundhage is there to bring back the playfulness and the creativity—to inject some fun.

The next major change comes by way of injury: Abby Wambach, top scorer, fearless leader, collides with a player in the last game before the Olympics. She writes about the moment in her memoir: "My mind, hyper-attuned, delivers its diagnosis: Both the tibia and fibula are broken. Another realization crests to the surface: The team leaves for the Olympics in five days, and I am not going to be on that plane. Inside my vortex of thoughts, depression buds and takes root. *Not now,* I think, and swat it away. Later I'll have plenty of time to tend to it and feed it and watch it grow, but now I have to be on my game. I have to be a captain." Being a captain means looking ahead, thinking about what needs to happen for the welfare of the team. In the ambulance, she calls Lauren Cheney: "Get ready, you're going. We need you." This moment illustrates just how much the "never defend alone" mindset had permeated Wambach's entire being. She wouldn't be on the field for her teammates, but they are still the first thing on her mind—even as she lays on a stretcher in an ambulance.

In her absence, who would rise to lead the team in the 2008 Beijing Olympics?

↓ Here, Lori "Chups" Chalupny bosses the midfield for the USWNT in their 2007 World Cup run. In 2008, she would score a memorable goal against Japan en route to the team's Olympic gold medal.

A year after she was controversially removed from the squad in 2007, goalkeeper Hope Solo (left) shares a gold-medal moment in Beijing with the woman who brought her back into the USWNT fold, new head coach Pia Sundhage.

In the 96th minute, Lloyd ropes in a shot from nineteen yards out. It is the world's first glimpse of a certain propensity to shine when it matters most.

Neither a water-logged field ↑
nor the Canadian defense
can slow down a determined
Carli Lloyd in the classic 2008
Olympic quarterfinal—a tightly
contested match that weather
delays prolong to more
than four hours.

Natasha Kai is the first Hawaiian to ever make the National Team. She grew up on the North Shore of Oahu and always had a surfboard and a ball in the back of her pickup truck. She got her first tattoo when she was eighteen, and her parents found out during a televised game when her shirt came loose during a diving header; the cameras zoomed in on her lower back and her grandpa froze the screen, took a picture, and sent it to her parents. When she left Hawaii, her father Benny, a famous musician in the islands, gave her an abalone-adorned ukulele that she brought with her to National Team camp. There, she learned to play on the bus rides and during the long hotel hours to steady herself as she, like the rest, fought for a spot. In overtime of the Olympic quarterfinals against Canada, Natasha Kai sprawls out—scoring a diving header similar to the one that got her busted for her tattoo years earlier. She sprints to the wing and dances, Boxx joining her step for step, arm gesture for arm gesture. All over the country, the Americans feast their eyes: The joy, the electricity—it is back.

In the semis against Japan, Hucles scores twice, then O'Reilly, then Chalupny—to make

it a definitive 4-2 victory. In the final, they face Brazil. For the first time in the history of the USWNT, they are expected to lose. These are the exact circumstances in which twenty-six-year-old, Jersey-girl Carli Lloyd thrives: She is most motivated by the opportunity to prove her doubters wrong. In the 96th minute, Lloyd ropes in a shot from nineteen yards out. It is the world's first glimpse of a certain propensity to shine when it matters most, to emerge from the blur of a game to score spectacular goals. The Americans win gold.

IN 2010, Shannon Boxx is doing her workout in the ocean air of the Strand, the sidewalk along Hermosa Beach: Run as hard as you can for five minutes, jog and recover for three, then repeat. She's midinterval when she runs into fellow Hermosa Beach local, Mia Hamm, walking with a double-stroller, twins in tow. "And even though she was my teammate and I know her well, she was—*is*—my role model, and you still get those little butterflies when you run into her," says Boxx. *How cool it is to see her in this next phase of life,* Boxx thinks. Hamm is deep into twins-mom life, but she still follows the team closely. She tells Shannon how well she thought she'd been playing and the two legends stand there together on the sidewalk, catching up. Mia gives Shannon some final words of encouragement—*Keep at it, you got this!*—and then takes off. Boxx has two Olympic gold medals, but there is one dream that has eluded the U.S. National team for more than ten years. As she inhales and exhales ocean air, passersby admiring her pace, there is one thing she's still after, what the entire team is after: a World Cup victory.

BY THE NUMBERS

51
Consecutive games without a defeat (the USWNT record), which lasted from December 8, 2004, until September 22, 2007. During the streak the U.S. won forty-three games and tied eight.

19
Number of wins Norway has over the USWNT, the most by any country. The Norwegians, however, have managed only one victory over the U.S. since 2003.

2
The lowest position of the USWNT in the FIFA Women's World Ranking, which debuted in 2003.

850
Percentage increase in sports bra sales, from 1998 ($412 million), before Brandi Chastain's shirtless World Cup celebration, to 2009 ($3.9 billion).

2
Players (Michelle Akers and China's Sun Wen) who shared the honor of FIFA Women's Player of the 20th Century announced in December 2000. Pelé and Diego Maradona were cowinners of the men's award.

OUTSIDE THE LINES

◀**Oct. 31, 2001:** Cable giants Cox Communications, Cablevision, Time Warner Cable, and Comcast are part of a $40 million investment in the WUSA professional league with USWNT players acting as the league cornerstones. The league would fail in 2003 due to a lack of corporate sponsorship.

◀**July 28, 2001:** Two years after the fact, men's soccer star Landon Donovan pays homage to Brandi Chastain's 1999 World Cup celebration by revealing a sports bra under his jersey after scoring in the MLS All-Star Game.

◀**Feb. 19, 2002:** Chastain and Men's National Team player Cobi Jones ring the opening bell at the New York Stock Exchange.

May 26, 2003: Just four months before the scheduled start of the tournament, FIFA relocates the 2003 Women's World Cup to the United States due to the SARS epidemic in China, the original host nation.

◀**Aug. 31, 2004:** Ten members of the gold-medal-winning 2004 team appear on *Late Night with David Letterman*, participating in "Top 10 Things I Can Say Now That I've Won a Gold Medal." Number 1 is Mia Hamm saying, "It's pretty clear who wears the pants in the family now, huh, Nomar?" referring to her husband, baseball star Nomar Garciaparra.

YEAR BY YEAR RESULTS

YEAR	2000	2001	2002	2003	2004	2005	2006	2007	2008	2009
W-L-D	26-6-9	3-5-2	15-2-2	17-2-4	28-2-4	8-0-1	18-0-4	19-1-4	33-1-2	7-0-1
Tournament Wins	G, ALG, U		G, U	ALG, FN	C, ALG, FN	ALG	G, FN, PQ	ALG, FN	O, C, ALG, FN, PQ	

ALG=Algarve Cup
ALB=Albena Cup
B=Brazil Cup
C=CONCACAF Women' Championship

CAN=Canada Cup
COL=Columbus Cup
F=Tournoi International Feminin
FN= Four Nations Tournament

G=CONCACAF Gold Cup
GG=Goodwill Games
I=CONCACAF Women's Invitational

NA=North America Cup
O=Olympics
PQ=Peace Queen Cup
Q=Chiquita Cup
S=SheBelieves Cup

T=Tournament of Nations
TRI=Tri-Nations Tournament
U=U.S. Women's Cup
W=Women's World Cup

MILESTONES

100TH CAP

MAY 31, 2000   **SHANNON MACMILLAN**
JULY 3, 2001   **CINDY PARLOW**
SEPT. 8, 2002   **LORRIE FAIR**
JUNE. 14, 2003   **TIFFANY ROBERTS**
JULY. 13, 2003   **CHRISTIE RAMPONE**
SEPT. 25, 2003   **KATE MARKGRAF**
JULY. 30, 2006   **ALY WAGNER**
JAN. 26, 2007   **CAT WHITEHILL**
SEPT. 22, 2007   **ABBY WAMBACH**
JULY 16, 2008   **LINDSAY TARPLEY**
AUG. 15, 2008   **SHANNON BOXX**
AUG. 21, 2008   **HEATHER O'REILLY**
NOV. 8, 2008   **ANGELA HUCLES**
MAR. 11, 2009   **HEATHER MITTS**

100TH GOAL

OCT. 10, 2004   **KRISTINE LILLY**
JULY 10, 2005   **TIFFENY MILBRETT**
JULY 19, 2009   **ABBY WAMBACH**

200TH CAP

APR. 8, 2000   **KRISTINE LILLY**
JULY 3, 2000   **MIA HAMM**
NOV. 11, 2000   **JULIE FOUDY**
OCT. 6, 2002   **JOY FAWCETT**
OCT. 22, 2003   **TIFFENY MILBRETT**
AUG. 12, 2008   **CHRISTIE RAMPONE**

300TH CAP

OCT. 16, 2005   **KRISTINE LILLY**

DECADE LEADERS 2000–2009

GOALS		WINS	
ABBY WAMBACH	101	**HOPE SOLO**	66
CINDY PARLOW	50	**BRIANA SCURRY**	52
KRISTINE LILLY	49	**SIRI MULLINIX**	24
MIA HAMM	44	**NICOLE BARNHART**	12
SHANNON MACMILLAN	38	**LAKEYSIA BEENE**	10

THE ALL-DECADE XI

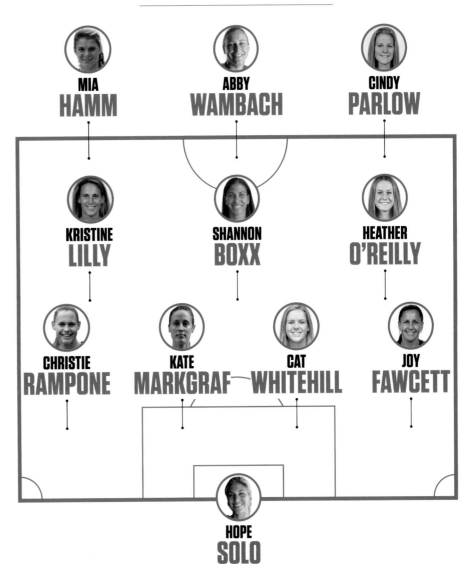

MIA **HAMM**   ABBY **WAMBACH**   CINDY **PARLOW**

KRISTINE **LILLY**   SHANNON **BOXX**   HEATHER **O'REILLY**

CHRISTIE **RAMPONE**   KATE **MARKGRAF**   CAT **WHITEHILL**   JOY **FAWCETT**

HOPE **SOLO**

Selected by a panel of current and former USWNT players, coaches, and members of the media. See page 254.

→ A U.S. wall (from left: Mia Hamm, Aly Wagner, Shannon Boxx, Abby Wambach, and Julie Foudy) goes up fast in Philadelphia to thwart a free kick in a 2004 friendly against Denmark.

Norway tries vainly to keep close tabs on Tiffeny Milbrett, who scores twice in the 2000 Olympic final in Sydney, but it is the U.S. that comes up short and has to settle for silver.

Down 2-1 with literally seconds remaining in the match the U.S. seemed destined to be receiving silver medals, or what Julie Foudy prefers to call them: White Gold. But Mia Hamm chased a long pass into the right corner. In reality, few players could reach the ball before it trickled out of bounds, and even fewer could launch a playable cross once they got to it. But Hamm could. And she did. From there, Milbrett found a way. At five-foot-two and the smallest player on the field, she leapt to reach Hamm's cross. Straining for what was possibly her personal best vertical jump and stretching her neck as long as it would go, Milbrett nodded the ball over Norwegian goalkeeper Bente Nordby for the unlikely equalizer.

TIM NASH, *It's Not the Glory*

→
Just days after being named to her first World Cup squad in 2003, Danielle Slaton dribbles through Costa Rican traffic during the fortieth game of her international career.

The reason I got involved in soccer was because I was running around the house breaking things like lamps and chairs. My parents said what's the next sport that's available and it was soccer. I joined the local AYSO league and I was the only girl on an all-boys team. At an early age I was able to see the cultural differences between what we tell little boys and what we tell little girls . . . the messages we tell them . . . what they can and can't do or are supposed to do. There is nothing weak about being strong . . . whether it's strong body or strong mind, and strong can be really sexy too and that's a good thing.

DANIELLE SLATON, NBC interview

Born in Memphis, Tennessee, Parlow sometimes registered in team hotels as "Elvis." She came to soccer as soon as she could stand up. Her oldest brother would put a ball at her feet as she learned to walk, and each step became an incipient dribble. "I'd take a step and fall," Parlow said, "sometimes I'd hit my head on the ball and fall backward and my brother would go, 'No cry, no cry.' He didn't want me growing up to be a girlie-girl."

She learned to strike the ball with her head because she was tall and because it was the thing to do among the boys in the neighborhood.

JERÉ LONGMAN, *The Girls of Summer*

Norway had reached the semifinals of every major woman's tournament until they were knocked out by high-flying Cindy Parlow and company in the 2003 World Cup quarters at Gillette Stadium in Foxborough, Massachusetts.

As an All-American junior at the University of North Carolina, the rugged young defender Cat Reddick (later Whitehill) becomes the only amateur chosen as part of the 2003 U.S. Women's World Cup roster.

The bad news about the USA's opening victory over Sweden in the 2003 World Cup was that Brandi Chastain broke a bone in her foot and was lost for the tournament. Catherine "Cat" Reddick stepped in and filled Brandi's role next to Joy Fawcett in the center of the defense. At twenty years old, Cat was the youngest player on the team. When the World Cup was over she would head back to school at the University of North Carolina, joining Lindsay Tarpley and Heather O'Reilly to help the Tar Heels to an undefeated season and another national championship. For now, she was enjoying the ride.

To those in Alabama, where she grew up, Cat would explain North Carolina was considered the North. She came from a football family, her dad having played at the University of Georgia. "When I told my dad I wanted to play soccer, he said, okay. Then he got a book on Coaching Soccer for Dummies, got out his clipboard and his Georgia Bulldogs megaphone, and coached my team," said Cat.

In the USA's next World Cup match, a 3-0 win over North Korea, Reddick scored twice in the second half to become the unlikely hero.

TIM NASH, *It's Not the Glory*

It took me three years to get a camp invite from the USWNT for the 2003 World Cup tryouts. And even then, since I was older than the average invitee and had a minimal pedigree, I was told I had "no chance" to make the team. "Come in, and we'll see how you compete against the best," I remember them telling me. "And then maybe you'll have a chance at the Olympic team in a year." It turned out to be a blessing in disguise. With nothing to lose, I played loose. And when I play loose, I play well. I played so well, in fact, that I forced my way onto the team — at the ripe old age of twenty six.

SHANNON BOXX, *The Players' Tribune*

Shannon Boxx earns the first of 195 caps and scores the first of her twenty-seven career goals against Costa Rica in 2003. Weeks later, she is named to the Women's World Cup 2003 All-Star Team.

FROM: CONGRESSIONAL RECORD

Speech of Hon. Fred Upton of Michigan In the House of Representatives
Tuesday, September 28, 2004

Mr. Upton: Mr. Speaker, I rise today to pay tribute to United States Olympic Women's Soccer player, Lindsay Tarpley, whose outstanding play helped the team bring home the gold in Athens. The grace and class that Lindsay and the entire women's soccer team demonstrated during their superb Olympic championship run is an inspiration to all of us.

In the 2004 Olympic gold medal game, millions of people around the world watched as Lindsay brilliantly scored the United States' first goal as the team went on to defeat Brazil 2-1. Her play throughout the tournament was marvelous and made the whole of southwest Michigan exceedingly proud.

↑ Lindsay Tarpley opens the scoring with this shot in the 2004 Olympic Final. Less than a week later, she returned to Chapel Hill to begin her junior season for the Tar Heels.

On a squad of mothers, [Heather] O'Reilly is still a daughter. "She's funny, she's naive, she's cute," says coach April Heinrichs. On the bus trip from Shanghai to Yiwu, site of the Norway win, the veterans talked dresses and dates with their young charge. Seven-year National Team member Cindy Parlow, twenty-four, who missed her prom to play in a match, told O'Reilly, "I'm living through you." More and more, the U.S. will be looking to her. In Sunday's 2–0 loss to China, O'Reilly came on in the second half and was a constant threat to score. Comparing her on-field development with that of her celebrated teammates, Heinrichs says, "She's more technical and more tactical [than they were] at eighteen. She has a one-versus-one personality but the ability to get others involved. Her self-esteem is shockingly ahead of her peers'."

MELISSA SEGURA, *Sports Illustrated*

→ At nineteen years old, Heather O'Reilly was the youngest player on the 2004 Olympic roster. Here she plays with the ruthless swagger that would mark her fourteen years with the team.

The old machine was sputtering. A newer model was surging, or so it seemed. Once, then twice, a Brazilian shot pinged off the left post of the United States goal. The score was tied in the women's gold-medal soccer match, and Brazil seemed poised to break through.

In the middle of the maelstrom, Abby Wambach considered what was happening. Maybe, she thought, those shots hit the posts for a reason. Maybe those quick Brazilian legs were not supposed to score goals. Maybe the story would end the right way.

"I think we all know who deserved to win today," said Wambach. "By whatever grace it was, they hit the posts, and we had a few chances. There was no other outcome possible for us. That's just the way it was meant to be."

Wambach seized her chance in the 22nd minute of overtime, plunking a header into the net to break the tie and send the United States to a 2-1 victory. The gold medal ensured that the old guard of American women's soccer would go out together as champions.

TYLER KEPNER, *New York Times*

As it does for most of her record-breaking year, the ball bounces the right way for Abby Wambach during the 2004 Olympic gold medal game against Brazil.

Tony DiCicco is best known as the coach of the 1999 World Cup champions, but he also "discovered" Christie Rampone just as she was preparing for her senior basketball season as star point guard for Monmouth College in West Long Branch, New Jersey, and considering a future in the newly formed WNBA. Though hoops was her first love, Rampone happened to be a record-setting forward for the college's soccer team. She was playing a game against Central Connecticut State in New Britain, Conn., when DiCicco had a look and came away astounded at her speed and athleticism.

"She's so far above everybody else on the field athletically," he thought. "Is it because she is truly that great an athlete, or could it be the level she is up against?"

His hunch was the former, and he was right. He sent a fax inviting Rampone—then Christie Pearce—into a National Team training camp. Pearce's roommate was Mia Hamm. Pearce could barely fathom where she was. DiCicco could barely fathom what he'd found.

"It's an incredible story, and it's not just her longevity," DiCicco says of USWNT captain Rampone and her 311 caps. "I think she's one of the two best defenders (along with Joy Fawcett) the United States has ever had."

WAYNE COFFEY, *New York Daily News*

←
Nobody in USWNT history has played more minutes (3,067) in a single year (2008) than longtime captain Christie Rampone (seen here against Australia).

The longer I was on the National Team, the more I realized that my personality was different from many of my teammates. I wasn't outgoing and bubbly; I struggled socially in big groups. I didn't want to go to movies or to dinner in huge throngs that involved endless planning and negotiations and waiting around. I found it exhausting to be with twenty other women all the time—at training, on the bus, at every meal. I had a difficult time being social twenty-four hours a day. Other girls easily shared their innermost thoughts about boyfriends and family and personal issues, while I liked to keep my private business private. I felt the same as I had in high school: unwilling and unable to play the "social girl" game. But I knew that when I said, "No thanks" to an invitation and closed my hotel room door so I could read or talk to my dad on the phone and re-charge my energy supply, people thought I was being unfriendly.

"People just don't feel like they know you, Hope," Aly Wagner once told me. I knew that was true. It had been the same in high school and college. My lack of comfort in group situations made me feel as if I was dysfunctional, missing one of my X chromosomes . . . . I didn't know that made me a black sheep.

HOPE SOLO (WITH ANN KILLION),
Solo: A Memoir of Hope

← A leaping Hope Solo punches away a shot in heavy traffic against Canada in the 2008 Olympics. That year the USWNT went 23-1, thanks in large part to Solo, who recorded clean sheets in over half the games.

As their team practices during a hot and humid Beijing summer day before the 2008 Olympic tournament, Heather O'Reilly (left) and Lindsay Tarpley find a novel way to play it cool.

As the youngest of seven children, Abby Wambach grew up playing the role of family tackling dummy. By age seven, she was routinely lashed into hockey pads so her brothers could fire pucks at her in the neighborhood cul-de-sac. Even at meals, she was on defense: She learned to quickly bite each French fry in half so that her siblings wouldn't raid her plate. Twenty years later, Wambach offers this sage life lesson: "Always cut your underwear a little so that when your brothers hang you on the doorknob, it will tear away easier."

Now five-foot-eleven and 175 pounds, Wambach gets pushed around by no one. She's the most imposing scorer on the United States national soccer team.

JERÉ LONGMAN, *New York Times*

→
Abby (Air) Wambach goes above and beyond a Norway defender in the 2007 World Cup third-place game, ultimately scoring two goals in the 4-1 U.S. win.

At all times I'm attuned to where the ball is, like a pointer dog identifying its prey, and I am running as fast as I ever have, gaining speed. Cheers from the crowd rise up to follow me and as I am about to make my move, I am stopped by the point of my opponent's knee. It stabs at my leg with super-human ferocity. I feel my left leg leave itself. I am on the ground, now, with a clear view and see that my foot and my thigh are turned in opposite directions, as if in a disagreement that can never be resolved.

ABBY WAMBACH, *Forward: A Memoir*

↓ Abby Wambach writhes in pain after suffering a broken tibia and fibula in July 2008. The surgery that follows includes the insertion of a titanium rod and sidelines the high-scoring forward for more than ten months.

Losing Abby's presence, I think we all had to step up and fill what was missing, but not one person could do it alone. They gave me my piece of the puzzle and gave everyone else their pieces, and we just all had to bring that out at our maximum capacity.

ANGELA HUCLES,
ussoccer.com

→
Called on to replace the injured Abby Wambach, Angela Hucles scored four goals in a six-game span at the Beijing Olympics.

The starting eleven came together in Shanghai before a hard-fought 1-0 victory over Africa champion Nigeria in the 2007 World Cup. Lori Chalupny's sliding goal just fifty-seven seconds in was the fastest score in U.S. World Cup history, and it was enough to send the Americans to the quarterfinals. Back row from left: Abby Wambach, Chalupny, Kate Markgraf, Hope Solo, Cat Whitehill, Kristine Lilly. Front row from left: Stephanie Lopez, Heather O'Reilly, Carli Lloyd, Shannon Boxx, Christie Rampone.

The "clutch player" has always held a special place in the hearts of sports fans: Reggie Jackson, Jerry West, Tiger Woods. Then there is "A-Rod"—no, not Alex Rodriguez. This is USC's Amy Rodriguez, newly minted member of the U.S. Women's Soccer Team. Rodriguez, twenty-one, has already staked her claim as one of the United States' best goal scorers.

"She is one of the fastest players on our team, and I think as long as we can keep putting her in positions where she can score goals for us she'll continue to do so," said Abby Wambach. "What I found with Amy is that when she gets those opportunities and chances she capitalizes on them."

Speed is what she is all about, and Rodriguez gives U.S. Coach Pia Sundhage a different dimension. Veteran U.S. defender Kate Markgraf sums it up this way: "She is so fast you can't stay with her. She reminds me of Tiffeny Milbrett and Marta. If you let A-Rod turn you [with the ball], you're fried."

A National Player of the Year in high school, the five-foot-four Rodriguez was called up to the full National Team in January and in June became the second-youngest player selected to the Olympic squad, for whom she scored five goals, three of them game-winners.

"I think it's an exciting time to be Amy Rodriguez," Wambach said, "especially if she keeps scoring these goals for us."

LUCAS SHAW AND PHILIP HERSH, *Los Angeles Times*

↑ In addition to scoring this goal against New Zealand in group play, Amy Rodriguez assisted on Carli Lloyd's rocket past Brazil's keeper in extra time, the only score of the 2008 gold medal game.

There are the tattoos, body decorations that rival David Beckham's assortment of odd images in odd places. [Natasha Kai] has nineteen of them. The twenty-five-year-old Hawaiian striker is a free spirit, a surfer, a singer, a dancer. She is also an Olympic semifinalist on the U.S. women's soccer team, just one victory shy of winning a medal at the Beijing Games.

It was Kai's goal in the 101st minute on Friday that earned the U.S. team a 2–1 overtime victory over Canada. The dramatic goal came in a game played during a driving rain amid lightning strikes that caused a one-hour-thirty-nine-minute delay. Midfielder Shannon Boxx floated in a cross from the left and Kai, who entered the match at the start of overtime, sprinted toward the goal and stooped to head the ball powerfully past Karina LeBlanc.

Los Angeles Times

→
On the heels of her game winner in overtime of the 2008 Olympic quarter-finals, Natasha Kai is called on for fresh legs in OT to help the U.S. win the gold, or as she put it afterward, the "bling."

We are in Brazil's end, six minutes into overtime of the 2008 Olympic final. I hold off a defender and back-heel the ball to Amy Rodriguez, who takes a touch and threads it back to me under heavy pressure. I see a sliver of space, explode forward, and let fly with my left foot, the ball launching low and hard, a skidding one-hopper heading toward the right corner. Barbara, Brazil's keeper, dives to her left. She might get a fingernail on the ball. She cannot stop it. The ball is in the Brazilian goal, and I am running toward my teammates, arms pumping, joy pouring from me.

All I can think is: This is why I train. This is why I run those hills in Laurel Acres, do those 800 repeats, the ninety-minute distance runs. It's why I do all the body weight exercises, why my trainer James and I keep pushing for more and better ways to get me fitter. I empty the tank in training, so the tank is never empty in games.

CARLI LLOYD (WITH WAYNE COFFEY),
When Nobody Was Watching

Carli Lloyd wheels away in triumph following her golden goal to defeat Brazil in the 2008 Olympic final.

2010s

AFTER LETTING THEIR CROWN SLIP IN THE PREVIOUS DECADE, THE U.S. WOMEN REASSERTED THEIR SUPREMACY BY WINNING TWO WORLD CUPS THANKS TO SUPERSTARS LIKE CARLI LLOYD AND MEGAN RAPINOE AND A NEW GENERATION WHO WERE "BADASSES" BOTH ON AND OFF THE FIELD.

→
Carli Lloyd's soaring talent is on display here after she score her first World Cup goal during a 2011 group stage match against Germany.

BLOOD AND GUTS

BY **GWENDOLYN OXENHAM**

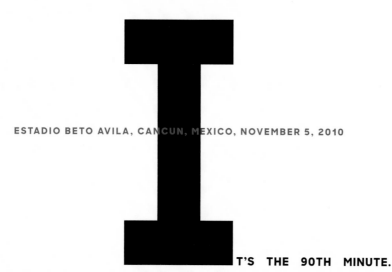

ESTADIO BETO AVILA, CANCUN, MEXICO, NOVEMBER 5, 2010

IT'S THE 90TH MINUTE.
A World Cup berth is at stake. The U.S. is losing to Mexico, and Abby Wambach has just smashed temples with a Mexican player and split her head open. Now blood's gushing down the side of her face.

Today, in the era of head trauma awareness and concussion protocols, Wambach would never be allowed to keep playing; then, Wambach doesn't appear to even considering subbing out. She shouts for the trainers to staple her up and get her back out there. On YouTube, you can watch a clip of the Deportes broadcast: the cameras zoom in for a tight close-up of Wambach's face—capturing each drip of blood, every staple. The comments on YouTube are all variations of "Holy shit— she's getting staples in her head and barely flinching!" and "This is why she's my favorite player." Football coaches at the University of Florida, her alma mater, later play this clip to their team to illustrate what it means to be tough.

Determined to avenge the team's heartbreaking loss to Japan in the 2011 World Cup final, Hope Solo and the USWNT battle ferociously in the rematch a year later and claim Olympic gold.

U.S. centerback Becky Sauerbrunn, then a rookie, recalls watching from a few feet away: "They're just like—doosh, doosh—shooting staples into her forehead. And then she runs out there and keeps heading the ball as though nothing has happened. And I was just like, *Oh, so that's what it's like to be on this team.*"

But toughness doesn't win them the game; the United States loses to Mexico for the first time in history. Which sends them into an intercontinental playoff with Italy. The number-one-ranked team in the world is in jeopardy of not qualifying for the World Cup; they are fighting for the last remaining spot.

PADUA, ITALY, NOVEMBER 20, 2010

The number one ranked team in the world is in jeopardy of not qualifying for the World Cup; they are fighting for the last remaining spot.

THE UNITED STATES hasn't lost to Italy since those first years back in the 1980s, when they were still sewing the USA patches onto their jerseys themselves. But on November 20, 2010, the U.S. can't manage to pull away. It's 0-0 in the 93rd minute. (It's worth mentioning that the sideline ref has indicated two minutes of stoppage time—which means the game is one minute into the red.) Carli Lloyd sends a beautiful long ball up the field where a new kid, Alex Morgan, is streaking toward goal. Morgan finishes with consummate ease, winning the game; it's the first glimpse of a player who, like Lloyd, has the rarest of gifts—she scores when it matters most.

Seven days later, in the second leg of the playoff, an Amy Rodriguez goal seals the berth to the World Cup. These are crucial World Cup qualifiers yet the Mexico game isn't even televised in the U.S. But the lack of visibility adds to the intrigue: in the shadows, mysterious cosmic forces are swirling, gathering force. These matches foretell what is to come over the next decade: High drama. Guts. Chaos. Dying-seconds reversals. Did-that-just-happen soccer. And you can bet they will catch—and hold—the attention of the world.

2011 WORLD CUP

ON JULY 4 WEEKEND, in a group game against Colombia, a midfielder with a platinum blond pixie cut subs in for the U.S. and ropes in an artful shot from outside the eighteen. She runs to the corner flag, grabs an on-field mic, gives it a tap, flashes a high-wattage grin, and belts out Bruce Springsteen's "Born in the U.S.A." Around the country, fans stare at the screen with dazed smiles, murmuring to themselves under their breath, "Hell-*o*, who are *you*?"

Meet Megan Rapinoe, aka "Pinoe," a kid from rural California who grew up with a Tom-Sawyer-esque childhood, fishing for crawfish in the creek and playing pickup for hours with her twin sister—until they heard their mother's wolf whistle. "She puts her pinkies in her mouth—you can just hear it forever," says Pinoe. "That was our call home." On the field, Pinoe's country-grown spirit and creativity is on full display.

↑ So dangerous is Tobin Heath in the open field that opponents, such as this German defender in the 2015 World Cup, try stopping her any way they can.

It's been over ten years since the U.S. Women have won a World Cup; in that stretch, the team has nearly fallen off the public radar. In the last World Cup, the USWNT made their earliest exit ever. Now, in 2011, it feels like encountering the team afresh; there's a brand-new cast of characters to discover: Besides Rapinoe, there's Alex Morgan—the player who saved the day in the Italy WC qualifier, a twenty-one-year-old Berkeley graduate with a gazelle-like run.

There's Tobin Heath, a ball magician with a messy ponytail, a hippie spirit, and tricks like we haven't seen from any American before her. She reads *Surfer* magazine on bus trips, paints in her free time, skateboards to class at UNC, and plays hallway soccer in her dorm.

These National Team successors all have crazy love for the game, along with star power and flair to spare—yet it's their performances in high-stakes games more than their alluring personas that come to captivate the world.

In the quarterfinals, Rapinoe again lights up the screen with a pass for the ages. The U.S. is playing Brazil, the team that embarrassed them in the semis of the last World Cup. They are, again, losing, 2-1 in the 121st minute. That's when Rapinoe launches the cross of her life, sending a forty-five-yard Hail Mary. Abby Wambach rises—powerful, commanding, like the masthead of a ship—and heads the ball home. It is the latest a goal has been scored in World Cup history. Wild, stunned celebrations ensue. Rapinoe runs madly, incoherently toward Wambach, crashing into her arms.

↑ A high-scoring forward her entire career, O'Hara, seen here against North Korea at the 2020 Olympics, was re-deployed at outside back, a position she hadn't played at any level until a year before.

In the wake of Wambach's monstrous header, the U.S. is back in the public eye—trending on Twitter and all over Facebook.

In the ensuing shootout, goalkeeper Hope Solo's intense green eyes stare down the Brazilians. The daughter of a periodically homeless Vietnam vet who taught her how to play and would sometimes camp in the patch of woods beyond her soccer field, she's about as fierce as they come. Now she makes a diving, clutch save, which puts the fate of the Americans on the right foot of Ali Krieger, who's taking the final penalty kick. Like the rest of the players, Krieger has a compelling story: In college, she almost died from a pulmonary embolism, blood clots in her lungs. She worked her way back onto the field and resurrected her career while playing in Germany. Now she steps up to the spot and lashes the ball into the bottom corner; the U.S. wins what is by far the most exciting quarterfinal in women's World Cup history.

In the wake of Wambach's monstrous header, the U.S. is back in the public eye—trending on Twitter and all over Facebook, splashed across media ads, featured on *SportsCenter*, the talk of living rooms and bars around the country. And the mania only amps up as the team dispatches France 3-1 in the semis. It's on to the final, where they face Japan, a team reeling from tragedy—tsunamis and a nuclear meltdown having devastated their country just weeks earlier. In preparing his team, the Japanese coach shows footage of the wreckage, his message clear: They are playing to lift their nation.

And they do. Twice. In regulation and then again in overtime. In the 117th minute, Homare Sawa, team captain, scores on an acrobatic, lunging flick—which sends the game to penalties. The Japanese do not miss.

While Americans love winners, if there is ever a final to lose, this is it. The Japanese players collapse on top of each other, and seeing the jubilant disbelief on Sawa's face, it's impossible for anyone, U.S. fans included, not to be moved. Women's soccer turns out to be about so much more than just sports. The post-tournament global consensus is: We're all in.

THERE'S ONE QUALITY that runs through the entire U.S. team: audacity. Here's a story—one that, as Stanford coach Paul Ratcliffe puts it, "will tell you everything you need to know" about USWNT defender Kelley O'Hara.

For preseason, the Stanford women's team was in Hawaii. On their morning off, Ratcliffe took a walk with his family on one side of the beach, while the team sat on the other side, staring across the water at an island off in the distance. O'Hara idly wondered to her teammates whether it'd be possible to swim to it. "No way, no chance": That's how they responded. But those words, to Kelley, were like a dare: She and her teammate, Ali Riley, took off swimming across the Pacific Ocean. "When I got back, all the girls were sitting down, kind of laughing and looking uneasy," says Ratcliffe. "I was like, 'Uh, what's up?' That's when they pointed out two tiny flecks swimming out in the water, en route to an island that is *far* away—I'm talking like far, far out. And I'm responsible for these girls, and I'm panicked. When I told the Hawaii coach about it, he says, 'Yeah, people die doing that.'"

O'Hara and Riley got stung by jelly-fish; their legs were on fire. "We wanted to prove them wrong," says O'Hara. "And we did...but it was not one of my smarter life decisions. When we made it back, we were thankful we were still alive."

That quality—believing it's possible even when no one else does—is what defines the USWNT. Kelley O'Hara plays every second of the 2012 Olympics. Another new face is Sydney Leroux, who scores five goals in a qualifying game against Guatemala; her Twitter page reads, "I kick balls for a living."

And if you think there's no chance the Olympics could be as exciting as that previous World Cup, you'd be wrong.

The semifinal may be the greatest Olympic game of all time: Canadian

That quality— believing it's possible even when no one else does — is what defines the USWNT.

↓ Ali Krieger, who plays every minute of all six U.S. matches at the 2011 World Cup, always put her body on the line, as she does here against Japan.

Hope Solo trains her death stare on a Japanese opponent who is set to take a penalty kick in the epic shootout that decides the 2011 World Cup final.

captain Christine Sinclair scores first. Rapinoe answers: 1-1. Sinclair scores *again*; Rapinoe answers: 2-2. Sinclair scores for the *third* time; this time, Wambach answers. It's 3-3 heading into double overtime. Shots hit the crossbar, shots hit the post—both keepers make ridiculous saves—and in the 123rd minute of overtime, Alex Morgan, again, scores a last-second game winner: The U.S. wins. In the final, they face the team that broke their hearts in the World Cup a year ago.

A pattern emerges: In finals, something possesses Carli Lloyd. When she moves down the field, it's with absolute assuredness, conviction, a certain glint in her eye—like she has seen it all ahead, like she always knew what would happen: That she would score two goals and the Americans would win gold, their third Olympic gold medal in a row.

If, for a while, this National Team has been eclipsed by the fame of the 99ers, now they've come into their own. "We're not them," says Pinoe, "but we wouldn't be here without them." On the plane ride home from the Olympics, spotlight shining upon them, Pinoe makes the decision to come out publicly. "I feel like sports in general are still homophobic, in the sense that not a lot of people are out.... People want—they *need*—to see that there are people like me playing soccer for the good ol' U.S. of A.," she tells *Out* magazine in July of that year.

All the players on this team are unapologetically themselves. Anything goes: Wear pink pre-wrap and a ponytail—or a crew cut. Pose nude, or don't. Head to the stands postgame and kiss your husband—or kiss your wife. Wear a tuxedo to the ESPYs—or wear a backless dress. Be gay, be straight, come out, or stay private. They send a resounding, intoxicating message: Be proud of whoever you are.

On the crest of this glorious wave, in 2012, U.S. Soccer launches a third attempt at a professional league, the National Women's Soccer League (NWSL). In order to keep the league afloat, starting salaries for non-National Team players are meager—$6,500. But it's a beginning; like the 99ers before them, they too fight for a league, to build something that will last.

2015 WORLD CUP

ON THE STUBHUB CENTER practice field in Carson, California, a couple of months ahead of the 2015 World Cup, Abby Wambach walks out in neon Wayfarers, singing the Eurythmics: *I travel the world and the seven seas, everybody's looking for something....* Wambach, the most prolific scorer in international soccer, winner of two gold medals, and 2012 FIFA World Player of the Year, has, in fact, traveled the world

↑ Carli Lloyd exults after scoring the second of her three goals in the 2015 World Cup championship game in Vancouver. The sixteen-minute hat trick was the first ever in a women's final.

← Instilling a fierce intensity and an unshakeable bond among her players, Jill Ellis became the winningest coach in USWNT history while leading the team to two World Cup titles and twice being named FIFA World Coach of the Year.

and the seven seas in pursuit of the one dream that has eluded her: a World Cup title. Coach Jill Ellis is now at the helm. The feeling in the air? *This one is ours.* All those young kids from the 2011 World Cup are now seasoned, confident. And for Wambach, as well as Shannon Boxx—this is their final shot.

The U.S. defense is virtually impenetrable: They allow only one goal in the first six games and go on a 513-minute shutout streak. In front of Hope Solo, Becky Sauerbrunn, and Julie Johnston (now Ertz) anchor the backline. Sauerbrunn is a calm, technically assured orchestrator, while the rookie Johnston is scrappy and exuberant, a revelation who delivers one crunching tackle after another, while also, somehow, pressing forward.

A new addition to the U.S. offense is Christen Press, all-time leading goal-scorer at Stanford, who has won one award after another for her marksmanship. ("All four years of high school we called her 'The Boot,' says her best friend, Nima Majd. "It started because we were at her house and saw this golden boot, and we were like, 'Uh, what the hell is that?'"). Press scores in the first match against Australia.

If you think there's no chance the Olympics could be as exciting as that previous World Cup, you'd be wrong. The semifinal may be the greatest Olympic game of all time.

It's a fraught social climate, a tense moment in time and culture, where so much is happening off the field—and here is when their audacity really comes into play.

In the semis, the team hits its stride: with a resounding 2-0 win over a powerhouse German side. In the finals, with 25 million watching on TV, they once again face Japan. That thing possessing Carli in Olympic finals? Turns out it's *all* finals. In one spectacular sixteen-minute tear, Carli scores three times, and that third one, especially, is a wonder—she beats a player and then has the gall to chip the keeper from half-field. The game feels extraordinary, otherworldly—a euphoric shower of goals raining down from the heavens. The USWNT are done with last-second scrambles—now they win emphatically, with ease. Finally, Wambach and Boxx have their World Cup title.

After the tournament, when they visit the White House, President Obama says, "This team taught all America's children that playing like a girl means you're a badass."

BEING A BADASS extends beyond blood and guts on the field. It's that signature audacity—the nerve to speak out and not "just stick to sports." The 99er generation taught them to use their platform to shake up the world and that's what they aim for: They're icons, social activists who are unafraid to make waves.

On September 4, 2016, before an NWSL game, three days after San Francisco 49ers quarterback Colin Kaepernick first knelt in protest of the treatment of Black Americans, Megan Rapinoe takes a knee in solidarity—the first prominent white athlete to do so. Within four years, athletes all over the world do the same. The USWNT emblazons the words "BLACK LIVES MATTER" on the U.S. warm-ups, and the team releases the following statement: "We wear Black Lives Matter to affirm human decency. This is not political, it's a statement on human rights." During gay pride month, they wear jerseys with rainbow numbers. Sexual orientation, race, gender—the USWNT fights for equality across the board.

On the field, they rarely lose—which is no small feat considering how far the women's game has progressed worldwide: new professional leagues, corporate sponsorships, more technically skilled players. Other teams are now good— the U.S. is better. The depth of talent is so ridiculous it ensures that each player must fight to hold on to to her spot. While the Americans have always been known for their athleticism, now they are as likely to beat you through possession and combination play.

↑ Crystal Dunn, whose diminutive
stature belies her pugnacity,
grapples with a Dutch opponent
for a loose ball during the U.S.
Women's 2–0 victory in the 2019
World Cup final.

←
Just three minutes into a group
stage game with Sweden in the
2019 World Cup, Rose Lavelle
(left) nearly jumps out of
her boots after Lindsey Horan
(right) converts a Megan
Rapinoe corner kick.

They head into the 2019 World Cup on a twenty-one game win streak and are getting stronger with every match. Giving a youthful dynamism to the midfield are Lindsey Horan, who skipped college to go straight to the pros, and who can create as well as she can disrupt; Samantha Mewis, a six-foot-tall ball-winning force out of UCLA; and Rose Lavelle, a Cincinnati kid known for deft touches and imagination. Crystal Dunn narrowly missed the 2015 World Cup roster, but she has been on a tear ever since, leading the league in goals that year, winning MVP honors, showing that she belongs. Now she's a starting outside back. Collectively, they may be the most promising U.S. team of all time.

It's a fraught social and political climate, a tense moment in time and culture, where so much is happening off the field—and here is when their audacity really comes into play.

Not surprisingly it's Rapinoe who leads the way. Ahead of the quarterfinal against host France, she declares in a video released by *Eight by Eight* magazine that if the team wins the World Cup: "I'm not going to the f-ing White House." To which President Donald Trump tweets a challenge: "Megan should win before she talks."

And then Pinoe backs up her swagger, scoring the game-winners in both the quarters and the semis. "I think the bigger the spotlight, the more she shines," Jill Ellis says of Rapinoe. "I think the spotlights can burn people, but for Megan they show who she is."

When a penalty is awarded in the 61st minute of the final against the Netherlands, it's Pinoe who steps up to the spot. It's dizzying to imagine the pressure, the weight on her shoulders, Trump's voice and all of the trolls in her ear. It feels as though kicking this ball, scoring this goal, could win a social movement as much as a game. She takes a deep breath, wets her lips, strides to the ball—and buries it, side-netting, to score yet another game-winner.

↑ The U.S. players show the love to Megan Rapinoe, their difference-maker throughout the 2019 World Cup, after she scores the game-winning penalty kick against the Netherlands in the final.

Eight minutes later Rose Lavelle, the slight twenty-four-year-old who has gathered more and more poise throughout the tournament, flies through the midfield. She steals one bold touch forward after another, rolls it with her sole—playful, taunting, like she's considering what she'll do next—and then she's cutting left, cracking a left-footed rocket—*goal*. She drops to her knees and deliriously pounds the ground.

The United States wins.

THAT TWO-FINGER WHISTLE Megan's mother used to call her in for dinner back when she was a kid in Redding, California? It's still how Denise calls out to her daughter; that whistle is how they find each other after games. Megan walks to the stands and searches the thousands of faces for her mother's, listening. Denise blows hard on her pinkies, sometimes three or four times—and then Megan taps her ear, to say, *I can hear you, Mom.* In France, Denise swells with pride, staring down at this daughter of hers, who has had the most unimaginable month—answering the president of the United States, scoring one game-winner after another, carrying her team, challenging the world.

Now, postchampionship, the relief descends—*it's over.* Pinoe bear-hugs Lavelle, hoisting her off the ground. Draped in American flags, Allie Long and Christen Press wave to the crowd. Jessica McDonald passes the trophy back and forth with her eight-year-old son. Crystal Dunn, Julie Ertz, and Morgan Brian sprawl out on the grass, snow-angel style, moving their arms and legs in wide strokes through the gold confetti. They all embrace one another and cry.

In September, Rapinoe's named FIFA Player of the Year. In her acceptance speech, she stands before the crowd and urges her fellow athletes to do what she and her teammates—and every generation of the US Women's National Team—have always tried to do: "Use this beautiful game to change the world."

→
After a thirty-yard run that shreds the Dutch defense, Rose Lavelle launches a left-footed dart that seals the U.S. Women's second consecutive World Cup title.

BY THE NUMBERS

104
Consecutive USWNT home games without a defeat, a streak that was ended by China on December 16, 2015. That loss was the first since Denmark beat the U.S. on November 6, 2004.

41.8
Percent of Abby Wambach's record 184 career goals (77) that were scored with her head.

1-3
Inches of snow (according to various estimates) that fell during the USWNT's game against Mexico in Sandy, Utah, on March 31, 2010.

55
Yards traveled by a field goal kicked by Carli Lloyd at the Philadelphia Eagles training camp in August 2019, sparking rumors of an NFL tryout.

300K
People in the crowd at the ticker-tape parade in New York City's "Canyon of Heroes" to honor the 2019 Women's World Cup champions.

7
Years between Kristie Mewis's first and second USWNT goals. She scored on June 15, 2013, then again on November 27, 2020, after a six-year absence from the team.

OUTSIDE THE LINES

◀ **2011:** Appearing on *Dancing with the Stars,* Hope Solo makes it all the way to the semifinals before being eliminated on the paso doble & Argentine tango.

2015: According to EA Sports, the USWNT ranks as the twenty-third-most-played team worldwide out of more than six hundred women's and men' sides included in the video game *FIFA 2016.*

◀ **2015:** Taylor Swift invites members of the USWNT on stage at a concert in New Jersey the night after the ticker-tape parade celebrating their 2015 World Cup championship.

2016: Megan Rapinoe takes a knee before the national anthem, in support of San Francisco 49ers quarterback Colin Kaepernick's effort to call attention to police brutality and racial inequality.

2019: *Sports Illustrated* names Rapinoe its Sports Person of the Year, the first time in the magazine's sixty five-year history that an individual soccer player is honored.

HOW THEY DID IT

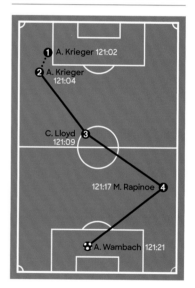

Abby Wambach's 122nd minute goal to tie Brazil in 2011 World Cup

YEAR BY YEAR RESULTS

YEAR	2010	2011	2012	2013	2014	2015	2016	2017	2018	2019
W-L-D	15-1-2	13-3-4	28-1-3	13-0-3	16-3-5	20-2-4	22-0-3	12-3-1	18-0-2	20-1-3
Tournament Wins	ALG	ALG, FN	O, C	ALG	C	W, ALG	S, C		S, C, T	W

ALG=Algarve Cup
ALB=Albena Cup
B=Brazil Cup
C=CONCACAF Women' Championship

CAN=Canada Cup
COL=Columbus Cup
F=Tournoi International Feminin
FN=Four Nations Tournament

G=CONCACAF Gold Cup
GG=Goodwill Games
I=CONCACAF Women's Invitational

NA=North America Cup
O=Olympics
PQ=Peace Queen Cup
Q=Chiquita Cup
S=SheBelieves Cup

T=Tournament of Nations
TRI=Tri-Nations Tournament
U=U.S. Women's Cup
W=Women's World Cup

MILESTONES

100TH CAP

NOV. 27, 2010	**CARLI LLOYD**
JULY 13, 2011	**HOPE SOLO**
DEC. 8, 2012	**AMY RODRIGUEZ**
MAR. 13, 2013	**RACHEL VAN HOLLEBEKE**
MAY 8, 2014	**LAUREN HOLIDAY**
APR. 4, 2015	**MEGAN RAPINOE**
MAY 10, 2015	**LORI CHALUPNY**
AUG. 19, 2015	**TOBIN HEATH**
JAN. 23, 2016	**ALEX MORGAN**
FEB. 21, 2016	**BECKY SAUERBRUNN**
SEPT. 15, 2017	**KELLEY O'HARA**
JUNE 12, 2018	**CHRISTEN PRESS**
MAY 16, 2019	**ALI KRIEGER**

200TH CAP

JULY 13, 2010	**KATE MARKGRAF**
FEB. 13, 2013	**ABBY WAMBACH**
MAR. 12, 2014	**HEATHER O'REILLY**
JUNE 26, 2015	**CARLI LLOYD**
AUG. 6, 2016	**HOPE SOLO**

300TH CAP

OCT. 24, 2014	**CHRISTIE RAMPONE**

100TH GOAL

APR. 8, 2018	**CARLI LLOYD**
APR. 4, 2019	**ALEX MORGAN**

DECADE LEADERS 2010–2019

GOALS		WINS	
ALEX MORGAN	107	**HOPE SOLO**	87
CARLI LLOYD	102	**ALYSSA NAEHER**	46
ABBY WAMBACH	83	**NICOLE BARNHART**	33
CHRISTEN PRESS	51	**ASHLYN HARRIS**	24
MEGAN RAPINOE	45	**JILL LOYDEN**	5

THE ALL-DECADE XI

MEGAN **RAPINOE**

ABBY **WAMBACH**

ALEX **MORGAN**

LAUREN **HOLIDAY**

CARLI **LLOYD**

JULIE **ERTZ**

CRYSTAL **DUNN**

BECKY **SAUERBRUNN**

CHRISTIE **RAMPONE**

KELLEY **O'HARA**

HOPE **SOLO**

Selected by a panel of current and former USWNT players, coaches, and members of the media. See page 254.

→ Megan Rapinoe's pose instantly
took its place alongside Brandi
Chastain's 1999 goal celebration
as an indelible image of the
U.S. Women's defiance and pride.

I'm not going to the f-ing White House.

MEGAN RAPINOE,
Eight by Eight magazine

Paris—It was fitting that the social justice activist Megan Rapinoe, the focus of unwanted presidential attentions before the game for her controversial White House comments, was the player to power the USA into a semifinal with England, scoring both goals in the Americans' 2-1 victory over the host nation. Rapinoe is more than a mouthpiece, she is, in the words of her teammate Kelley O'Hara, "a baller."

SUZANNE WRACK, *The Guardian*

The most famous women sports team of all time gave us familiar female characters. The graceful elegance of Mia Hamm, the brash flamboyance of Brandi Chastain, the vocal leadership of Julie Foudy, the maternal solidity of Joy Fawcett.

And then there was Kristine Lilly. The other member. Quiet, determined, hard working.

The one who ended up exceeding them all.

Lilly, thirty-nine, retired from competitive soccer on Wednesday, the last of the 99ers who changed sports history to say goodbye. She ends a career that was remarkable not only for its excellence and achievement but also for its ability to exist in the shadows.

"She's one of the most amazing athletes of our time," longtime teammate Chastain said. "The fact that I got to witness her up close was a life-altering experience."

ANN KILLION, *Sports Illustrated*

→
Kristine Lilly was a sixteen-year-old high school student when she made her debut for the U.S. By the time she retired in 2010, at thirty-nine, she had played 354 games for the National Team and won two World Cups and two Olympic golds.

Alex Morgan arrived late to the game, not starting club soccer until she was fourteen, an age when college coaches are already recruiting and she "wasn't even on their radar."

In the spring of her junior year at University of California, Morgan studied abroad in Madrid. "I went over there to totally immerse myself in the football culture." Every day, she'd head out to the futsal court with a ball and play by herself. Eventually, guys started coming around.

"They'd be in their forties and fifties, drinking vinotinto and smoking their cigarettes, and here I am, this white American girl who can barely get by conversationally," Morgan said. "The first couple minutes playing, they'd be like "Who is this girl? Oh, great.' They weren't expecting much from me."

They'd pass the ball to her, but they'd make sure to get it right back. But then Morgan would score from half court, bend the ball into the small goal, and their tune would change.

"They gave me a lot of respect," she said. "My time in Spain was my introduction to the world of football."

In the 2011 World Cup, the world was introduced to Morgan. She scored in the 82nd minute in the semifinal against France and then again in the final against Japan. In the 2012 London Olympics she scored the game-winning goal in the 123rd minute of the semifinal game against Canada. She finished the year with twenty-eight goals and twenty-one assists, joining Mia Hamm as the only American women to score twenty goals and collect twenty assists in the same calendar year.

GWENDOLYN OXENHAM, *SI.com*

MÖNCHENGLADBACH

The youngest player on the roster at twenty-one, Alex Morgan came off the bench for the 2011 World Cup. But while she hurdled the goalkeeper here, she can't lift the team over their bitter rivals Sweden in this group stage match, which the U.S. loses 2-1.

Disney would never have green lighted this script. Twenty-first-century audiences, raised on a steady diet of comic-book fare, are too worldly, too jaded to buy into a storyline so egregiously Hollywood. After all, this is a tale of nevers. Never before had Japan beaten the U.S. in twenty-five attempts; never before had the U.S. failed to win a World Cup match in which it scored first; and never before had the Americans failed to clear the last hurdle in the Women's World Cup once they reached it. The final score line will read Japan 2 (3) U.S. 2 (1), but in one of those gloriously rare moments in sports, it didn't matter which team won and which team lost.

You can talk all you want about Alex Morgan's cool, predatory strike following Megan Rapinoe's defense-shredding pass, Aya Miyama's fortuitous but well-taken equalizer, Morgan's laser cross to the most lethal forehead in sports (Abby Wambach's), Homare Sawa's seeing-eye 117th-minute Lazarus job executed with the kind of sublime skill normally reserved for YouTube videos. You can argue about substitution patterns, penalty-taking decisions, Hope Solo's left knee, and the vagaries of fortune.

But none of that matters. What we should remember today is how uplifting a great athletic event can be.

Sunday's final was a fitting capstone to the best, most competitive Women's World Cup ever played. As heartwarming a backstory as Japan brought into the tournament—team of destiny, looking to provide some joy to a country ravaged by the devastating tsunami and earthquake this past March—it wasn't the global response to the tragedy that won the World Cup for the Japanese. No, it was a magnificent display of resilience and fortitude, long considered indigenous American traits, that helped them overcome two seemingly insurmountable leads during the taut, pulsating 120 minutes of open play. And then, when the Nadeshiko were faced with the daunting task of scoring from the spot against the world's best goalkeeper, Hope Solo, they fell back on their greatest strength: technique. Yes, PKs are an excruciating test of nerve, but they also rely heavily on the players' ability to place the ball accurately and authoritatively out of the keeper's reach. Yet again, as they had done all tournament, the Japanese proved that they are the most highly skilled players in women's soccer.

DAVID HIRSHEY, *ESPN.com*

In one of the most memorable games in USWNT history, Alex Morgan (fourth from right) rises to the occasion in the 123rd minute with a header that beats Canada and sends the U.S. to the 2012 Olympics final.

←
Hope Solo registered more victories than any goalkeeper in USWNT history, but not even she can save this penalty kick in the 2011 World Cup final, which is won by Japan.

They were ready for this moment. And that moment came in the 123rd minute of a game packed with more drama than a high school hallway, when Team USA's young star forward, Alex Morgan, out-jumped, out-willed, and outlasted the Canada defense and headed in the second goal of her budding Olympic career to give the Americans a 4–3 win. It is a moment that will forever be remembered for propelling the U.S. Women's National Team into its fifth Olympic final. The moment the United States, after clawing from behind three times in eighty minutes, secured a rematch with 2011 Women's World Cup champion Japan, who relegated them to a silver medal that still haunts them. . . . The moment Alex Morgan scored the latest goal ever by a member of the U.S. Women's National Team.

In the end, the player they call Baby Horse, the woman who has been the workhorse of this Olympic tournament, came up big in the biggest of moments.

As she felt the weight of her teammates piling on her, the gravity of what she had just accomplished began to sink in and she shed a tear. "When we come together as a team, you can't break us," she said.

ALYSSA ROENIGK, *ESPN.com*

"I never get too hyped up too early before a game," says Alex Morgan. "I feel like that leads to having restless legs and mind. I do a lot of mental visualization and use breathing techniques just to kind of calm myself down."

PATRICK COHN,
soccerpsychologytips.com

→

Before a 2012 match against New Zealand, Alex Morgan (center) tunes out all distractions from bantering teammates (from left) Sydney Leroux, Lauren Cheney, Megan Rapinoe and Lori Lindsey. Morgan's pregame ritual works: She scores both U.S. goals in a 2-1 win.

I got my first call-up to the USWNT in April of 2012. Before I could exhale in relief—I had made it—I realized this was just the beginning. The USWNT isn't a place where you celebrate, put down roots, or relax. It isn't a place at all. Being on this team is an honor as well as a responsibility to my country and myself. Maybe it is another halfway point on the line to greatness. Because as long as you can look forward, you haven't arrived. What I do with this opportunity remains to be seen, but I know my success and my team's success depends on that forward motion.

CHRISTEN PRESS, *The Players' Tribune*

← After completing her third career hat trick in 2015, Christen Press was on a glide path to the ranks of the USWNT's top-tier goal scorers.

↓ Showing off her trademark trickery against a Costa Rican defender, Tobin Heath helps the USWNT roll up a combined 38-0 score against five CONCACAF opponents en route to the 2012 Olympics.

If the field is a chessboard, some players are rooks or knights. Tobin Heath is a queen, bound by no single role or path. She is faster than most and loses little of that speed with the ball at her foot. She has the fitness to maintain that pace after those defending her tire. She sees passing angles that others don't—or at least aren't willing to risk. She has the technical ability to bend in a shot from long distance and the body control, not to mention the fearlessness, to find a ball in traffic and finish with a back-heel in front of goal.

GRAHAM HAYS, *ESPN.com*

She came in when skies were gray following the ugly end to the 2007 World Cup [in which the U.S. was crushed by Brazil 4-0 in the quarterfinals]. And she very quickly made them happy with a positive laid-back approach that helped transform American soccer, both tactically and spiritually. The American game became more sophisticated under Sundhage. Bigger, stronger, fitter, and faster were replaced by smarter, slicker, quicker, and craftier. Players like star forward Alex Morgan and midfielders Carli Lloyd, Tobin Heath, Lauren Cheney, and Megan Rapinoe, who excelled at possessing the ball and creating chances with their skill and smarts, became featured options. "If you ask Pia to pull up clips of when you didn't succeed," said Morgan, "she'll say, 'Why don't you talk to another coach about that?' She's all about the positive."

When the language barrier was too much or words failed her, Pia sang. As the players gathered before a game, Sundhage told them to lie on the ground and close their eyes. Not to meditate or visualize, but to listen. She pulled out the guitar and sang from the heart, "The Times They Are A-Changin'," by Bob Dylan.

RAMONA SHELBURNE,
ESPN.com

→
After a stellar career coaching the US Women to two Olympic gold medals and compiling a record of 91 wins, 6 losses, and 10 ties, Pia Sundhage breaks down during an emotional farewell tribute in 2012 . Instead of a goodbye speech, Sundhage sings lyrics from the Bonnie Tyler tune "The Best" as the crowd chants, "Pia, Pia, Pia."

F***, we're about to go out in the quarterfinals. We're about to bomb out of this tournament right now. Please, please just give us one more possession. That's what was going through my head as the seconds ticked down on our 2011 World Cup run . . .

All we had to do was go a hundred yards and score—the soccer equivalent of a Hail Mary! In the two seconds that I had the ball at my feet I realized that I had only one option: Just get the ball into a dangerous area and get it there now. I took one touch to push the ball ahead and looked up quickly toward Brazil's goal. I saw a blur of four yellow jerseys and a green one (their goalkeeper) at that moment. I had to pass the ball to an invisible teammate. I knew that somewhere outside my peripheral vision Abby Wambach was sprinting furiously into the box. I didn't know where she was, but I knew where she would be. I had to hit it with my left foot. The problem is I'm not naturally left-footed and usually I don't have as much power as I do with my right. So I hit it pretty much as hard as I could.

A second later, I saw the net shake. Then the stadium shook. It was absolute pandemonium.

MEGAN RAPINOE, *The Players' Tribune*

↑ As the clock ticks down to the final seconds, Abby Wambach races to the far post and rises above the Brazilian defense for a header (later voted the greatest goal in American soccer history) that sends the U.S. Women to the 2011 World Cup semifinals.

↑ After her perfectly measured cross leads to an unforgettable 122nd minute goal against archrival Brazil, an ecstatic Megan Rapinoe leaps into Abby Wambach's arms.

My ear is anticipating the sound of the whistle, signaling our loss, our time to pack up and go home. I'm not sure if Megan sees me but she's running toward me and I know exactly what she'll do next: Look up and bomb it into the box. I creep into position, waiting to pounce. My mind gives me a last-second pep talk: Please don't miss. It would be the most epic failure in the history of the game . . .

The reflective memory of every past goal is packed into this second, informing the way I move—leaping off my right leg, slanting shoulders forward, matching the ball to my hairline, as inevitable as a puzzle piece finding its slot. That sweet familiar second of darkness. I open my eyes and know: I didn't miss. It's the latest goal ever scored in the history of the Women's World Cup.

ABBY WAMBACH, *Forward: A Memoir*

The U.S. women held off a late, desperate attack by Japan and won the gold medal 2–1 before 80,203 at Wembley Stadium, a record for Olympic women's soccer. They got two goals from forgotten midfielder Carli Lloyd, received a gift noncall from the referee, cleared a couple balls off the line, had two Japan shots hit the crossbar, watched goalkeeper Hope Solo make one acrobatic save after another—whatever it took, whenever, wherever, however.

Immediately after the final whistle, the U.S. players put on white T-shirts that said: "Greatness has been found." But, really, was it ever lost? They have struggled in recent World Cups, but this was their third straight gold medal and fourth out of five since the sport was added in 1996.

The players hugged and ran with the flag and waved to their families in the stands. As music pumped through the stadium, Pia Sundhage, the U.S. coach from Sweden, was alone at the center circle, playing air guitar and punching her fist into the night air.

MARK ZEIGLER, *San Diego Union-Tribune*

When the stakes are highest, Carli Lloyd is at her best. Here she scores against Japan in the 2012 Olympic final, which the U.S. wins 2-1.

← In one of the greatest Olympic performances by a goalkeeper, Hope Solo seems to defy the laws of physics in the pulsating 2012 final.

Although the U.S. Women won a gold medal four years ago in Beijing, they hankered for something more, something that justified their billing and popularity. And they were still scalded over their loss to Japan in the World Cup a year ago in a penalty-kick shootout.

What did they want? They wanted renown. "My point to this group is, you've got to win to become legends," Wambach said.

"I want the drama to be over," defender Christie Rampone said. "I want it to be exciting but not *that* exciting."

It wasn't—thanks to Carli Lloyd. The "often overlooked" midfielder came out of nowhere and practically knocked Wambach over when she saw Alex Morgan make a short cross 8 minutes 54 seconds into the first half. She sprinted in to cut off the pass with a head-banging goal. "Flew by Abby, flew by everybody," Lloyd said. "I was just determined to get that ball in the net." But Japan kept on coming, and that might have left U.S. goalkeeper Hope Solo exposed . . . She was a diving and deflecting demon, a one-woman highlight film and forever justified her outsized reputation. When Mana Iwabuchi took a direct shot from close range at the 82:33 mark, Solo went parallel. She batted it with both hands—and a legend was made.

Afterward they emerged from their showers with American flags wrapped around their shoulders like shawls and twined around their necks like scarfs, signaling a new sense of possession.

SALLY JENKINS, *Washington Post*

"I play too far away from the goal to shoot but I really want to score," says Ertz. "We have world-class players whipping in these crosses and all I have to do is run as hard as I can at the ball. I'm not backing down . . . I've knocked my teeth out so many times. It's a good thing my dentist is my uncle."

GRANT WAHL, *SI.com*

←
As the USWNT's defensive anchor in midfield, Julie Ertz is known for her toughness but she is also a go-to offensive threat, as she demonstrates here with a goal against Spain.

→
A nasty collision in the 2019 final against the Netherlands does not keep Becky Sauerbrunn off the field for long. The U.S. captain returns after two minutes to lead her team to its second straight World Cup title.

Like many on the USWNT, Sauerbrunn was a fanatical trainer: "I'd kick the ball up on a slanted roof and then wait for it to come down, and I'd do that for hours after school, and the perfectionist in me would have to do twenty in a row perfectly. Or I would dribble around lawn chairs and I would have to do it in one touch, and it would have to be twenty that were absolute perfection or I wouldn't allow myself to go inside."

Beyond being driven, she was also tough—due in large part to her role as her older brothers' "guinea pig." Among other indignities, they'd duct-tape plywood to her arms and take slap shots at her.

"Aside from physically toughening me up, they made me mentally stronger," says Sauerbrunn. If she cried, they'd call her a baby. If she said ow a little too loudly, hoping that her mom and dad would hear, they'd hit her harder, having caught on to her tactics. "I learned how to take it. It taught me how to not really rely on other people to solve my problems. I think that kinda stayed with me."

Her tolerance for pain came in handy during her first National Team cap against Canada. In the second half, Sauerbrunn went up for a challenge in the air and the Canadian player attempting to flick the ball instead flicked Becky's nose. Blood was "gooshing" down her face, and when a nearby teammate caught sight of her, looked at her with horror and told her to get off the field. The team doctor reset the nose right there in the locker room. Becky played in the next game with a "McGyver-like mask" made out of random materials they happened to have on hand in the training room—a contraption with the same industrious, ramshackle style as the plywood-hockey ensembles her brother would fashion for her as a kid.

GWENDOLYN OXENHAM, *U.S. Soccer.com*

The body that Sydney Leroux claims she used to hate is now a means of self-expression. It is a sketchbook, a story. She inked it, she pushed it, she put it on display. On Instagram, she appears in tiny bikinis, or posing with her puppy, or goofing off. She posed nude in *ESPN The Magazine*'s 2013 Body Issue. "I think a lot of females struggle with the way they look, and I wanted to show that everyone's body is different," she said. "I'm not going to say I've never struggled with how I look, but I've reached a point in my life where I'm happy with who I am." After she scored a goal in the Olympic quarterfinals against New Zealand, her face appeared in newspapers around the world, the picture of joy. She became the team's symbol of freedom and individuality.

She may be the future of American soccer, and perhaps even a generational figure in the culture. But it remains to be seen whether she can define its present—or whether she'll even have the chance.

Then came the World Cup tune-up match against Mexico, in Carson, California, on a lovely mid-May night. Alex Morgan was out with a bone bruise in her knee. Leroux got the start. And in the 28th minute, she got the ball. Receiving a pass through the middle from Megan Rapinoe, timing her run to stay right at the edge of onside, she surged into the box, dodging the diving keeper, and, just a foot or two before the end line, took a sharp-angled shot. The ball flew across the goal line and into the far side of the net. She'd go on to score again in the second half, running onto a Lauren Holiday pass over the top and rounding the keeper before hitting the back of the net.

"She's the most competitive person I've worked with, mentally and physically," Jill Ellis said. "She's been through a lot. When it's harder for her is when she's better."

LOUISA THOMAS, *Grantland*

← Sydney Leroux's 87th-minute goal—her first in an Olympics—helps send the U.S. past New Zealand and into the semifinals of the 2012 London Games.

↓ Julie Ertz (19) and goal-keeper Hope Solo can only look on helplessly as Meghan Klingenberg (right) leaps to the rescue against Sweden in the 2015 World Cup. Official replays confirm the five-foot-two defender's header off the crossbar never crosses the goal line.

Winnipeg, Manitoba—Meghan Klingenberg is a University of North Carolina grad who happened to be standing on the left post of the U.S.'s goal on Friday night when she made one of the most important goal-line clearances in U.S. World Cup history.

It made you think of Kristine Lilly, a University of North Carolina grad who happened to be standing on the left post of the U.S.'s goal in the 1999 final when she made one of the most important goal-line clearances in U.S. World Cup history.

What did both players say afterward? The exact same thing.

"Just doing my job."

Left back Klingenberg is the shortest player on the team at five-foot-two, but she can sky when she wants to. Teammate Julie [Ertz] said she thinks the Artist Known As Kling has the highest vertical jump on the team, and Kling wasn't going out of her way to deny that on Friday after the U.S. and Sweden played to a scoreless draw.

"When you're this short," she said, "you have to be able to make up for it somehow."

The play that saved the U.S. came out of a corner kick in the 76th minute, as Sweden's Caroline Seger rifled a shot that was heading to the upper corner. U.S. goalie Hope Solo had no chance. But Klingenberg rose from her spot on the post and headed the ball off the underside of the crossbar and clear.

GRANT WAHL, *SI.com*

Because the terms surrounding U.S. women's soccer are always so complex and so doubled—thanks to the legacy of 1999, the split in the fan base, the uphill climb faced by women's sports in general, and every other factor—the identity and destiny of the entire program can seem to turn on one moment, one goal, in an amazingly transparent way. Is the balance right? Are we winning? Are we selling shirts? Are we inspiring girls? Are we the best in the world? So often, all of those questions come down to this: Did Abby score?

BRIAN PHILLIPS, *Grantland*

The USWNT is locked in a tight 2015 match against Nigeria, Abby Wambach strikes in the 45th minute, scoring the only goal in the U.S. victory.

Vancouver, British Columbia—It took a timely suspension, of all things, to put the United States in position to win the Women's World Cup. Had Lauren Holiday not been absent through yellow card accumulation entering the quarterfinals, the U.S. might not have beaten Japan, 5–2, in the final on Sunday.

That suspension led to Morgan Brian replacing Holiday in central midfield for the final three matches, even after Holiday was restored to the lineup and repositioned on the flank. Coach Jill Ellis discovered that Brian allowed the team to be the best version of itself.

Beginning with a dominant performance in a 1–0 win over China, Brian, twenty-two, became the catalyst for the U.S. midfield's composure throughout the knockout round of the tournament. Holiday's absence caused coach Jill Ellis to retool her midfield, resulting in Brian providing a calming presence and some much-needed bite on both sides of the ball.

"The coaches asked her, 'Hey, this is the role we want you to play. Can you do it?'" said veteran defensive midfielder Shannon Boxx, who became a mentor to Brian. "She wanted to be on the field, just like everybody else, and she played her role tremendously. She kept disrupting attacks and winning balls in the midfield. No matter what, she always got a toe on it."

LIVIU BIRD, *SI.com*

→
In the 84th minute against Germany, Kelley O'Hara strikes a martial arts pose as she stabs the ball into the net to seal a 2–0 semifinal win for the U.S.

←
Given the opportunity to start for suspended teammate Lauren Holiday in the quarterfinals of the 2015 World Cup, midfielder Morgan Brian seizes her chance and turns in a rock-steady shift against China.

What if your ass never left the bench for four straight games, for roughly 360 minutes of watching and cheering and hoping your time will come? And what if, in the last major tournament before that, you played every minute of every game before having a gold medal draped over your neck?

Enter Kelley O'Hara, the 2015 World Cup super-sub extraordinaire, who everyone thought had vanished after her 2012 Olympic glory until an appearance against China and a ninja-kick goal against Germany. Over the last week or so, she proved that she's one of the best forwards-turned-defenders-turned-wingers in the world.

In 2012, she was groomed to be an outside back despite being one of the most prolific scorers in college, and she played the entire Olympics en route to the U.S.'s victory in the final over Japan. But ankle surgery in 2013 and the shuffling of head coaches left her in limbo for much of the past two years; she was no longer a forward, but not quite a defender, either.

U.S. coach Jill Ellis sat O'Hara for all of the group-stage games and in the round of sixteen against Colombia, but the U.S. struggled and Ellis turned to O'Hara in the quarterfinal game against China. She kept the width well and went at players before smashing her face on the back of a defender's head and exiting the game with a bloody nose. But she was back again in the 75th minute of the semifinal against Germany: a stutter step by Lloyd and—Was that Kelley?!—a leg flying into the six-yard box and a game-clinching goal.

ALLISON MCCANN, *Grantland*

"Lauren's awareness on the field sets her apart from a lot of other midfielders in the world," says USWNT captain Becky Sauerbrunn. "She just sees things, spaces and seams. And she's got the technical ability to execute whatever she sees and make it happen. That's really special. Some players may have the awareness but not the execution. She has both."

GRANT WAHL, *SI.com*

←
A longtime mainstay of the USWNT midfield, Lauren Holiday blasts what proves to be the 2015 World Cup-winning goal in the 5-2 victory over Japan.

Carli's a soccer icon everywhere in the world. If she were a male player in Europe, there would be statues of Carli Lloyd all over the place. I mean, streets would be named after her, complexes, stadiums, everything. That's how big she is.

CURRENT USWNT COACH VLATKO ANDONOVSKI

← Carli Lloyd's audacious bomb from the halfway line in 2015 shocks the world and leaves the Japanese goalkeeper on her back. The goal caps the greatest performance by a woman in a World Cup final.

Last summer Carli Lloyd scored three times in the first sixteen minutes of the World Cup final against Japan, the fastest hat trick in tournament history by a man or a woman. Now, seven months later, she recalls her third goal—an improbable fifty-four-yard kick from midfield—with assuredness and bemusement.

"When I got the ball at midfield, I took a touch. I looked up and saw the keeper off her line. I took another touch to prep. I just hit it. When it came off my foot, I knew it was perfect."

Then she laughs. It was a play that could never go right, except on the one day when nothing could go wrong.

Lloyd finally stepped to the forefront of women's soccer on that afternoon in July, but here at a Marlton, New Jersey, brunch spot called the Turning Point, she practically recedes into the background. She is not Serena Williams, granite sculpture of biceps and triceps. She is not Ronda Rousey, bulk and power. At five-foot-eight, her hair piled into a messy bun and sporting an unremarkable all-black warm-up suit, she could just as easily be your fitness-conscious roommate as a World Cup Golden Ball winner.

"The thing is," Lloyd goes on, "those sixteen minutes were thirteen years of hard, hard work."

HALLIE GROSSMAN, *ESPN The Magazine*

What makes Abby so remarkable is this: She's powerful and she knows it. She doesn't apologize for it, the way women are so often taught to do. She uses it—to level the playing field for women athletes and to change the story that we tell young girls about their own worth and potential.

—

HILLARY RODHAM CLINTON AND CHELSEA CLINTON,
The Book of Gutsy Women

←
Inspiring women around the
world with her unstoppable
American spirit, Abby Wambach
finished her amazing career
with 255 caps, a record 184 goals,
and a World Cup title in 2015.

At my very first National Team practice in 2011, I suffered an MCL injury and couldn't play the rest of the camp. I didn't get called back until 2014. In those three years away, I was all about hustling, grinding, and persevering. My motto became, "Be so good that they can't ignore me." And then before the 2015 World Cup, Jill Ellis told me that she was going to take someone more experienced than me. I watched them win and it was so hard, but I believed that my failures were preparing me to succeed. I wanted to show everybody: You didn't pick me, you doubted me. I'm going to make you regret that.

   I made the roster for the 2016 Rio Olympics, but we went out in the quarters, and it was heartbreaking not just for me but for the team. None of us wanted to experience that feeling ever again. At the end of 2018, I suffered another knee injury and had to sit out a couple of months. When I was finally called in for the last camp before the 2019 World Cup, I knew I couldn't take anything for granted. I just had to ball out and maximize every minute. I was coming for what's mine.

ALLIE LONG, *Positive University Podcast*

←
Allie Long was a late cut from the 2015 World Cup roster but four years later she completed a gutsy return to the team for its triumphant 2019 World Cup run.

I feel like what the U.S. Women's National Team stands for and what it represents is everything that we fight for all the time. It's all these women that have come before us. It's being role models for young girls. It's not always about patriotism, but it's always about what the team is, and the reason why I'm so honored is because of the women around me.

SAMANTHA MEWIS, *Snacks with Lynn and Sam podcast*

It took Lindsey Horan only three minutes to open the scoring and close out rival Sweden in this 2019 group stage World Cup match in France.

When Jill Ellis was remaking the National Team roster after the 2016 Olympic debacle and the ensuing end-of-cycle personnel changes, she called on Abby Dahlkemper, a four-time All-American at UCLA.

But just a few weeks after earning her first cap, Dahlkemper injured her toe and contracted a serious sepsis infection, which traveled up her leg. . . . Suddenly, everything was in doubt.

"Anytime there's an injury, you wonder, 'Am I going to be the same player?'" Dahlkemper said. "But this injury was different. I was just thankful to still have my leg. To be alive, and all that. It was a really humbling experience."

Dahlkemper underwent surgery to clean out the infection. She was bedridden for one and a half months and on intravenous antibiotics. When she finally was able to move around, her dominant right foot was in constant pain and her right leg was severely atrophied.

"I was starting from scratch," she said.

Yet she fought back. In the past five years, Dahlkemper has earned seventy six caps with the National Team. "She's got tremendous poise," Ellis said. "Her distribution, her quality of delivery. I think she's a natural playmaker in the back. She has a ruggedness about her, a physical dimension to her. I think you have to be brave in the back, and Abby's brave."

ANN KILLION, *San Francisco Chronicle*

←
Underrated and quietly efficient center-back Abby Dahlkemper was a constant presence in the 2019 World Cup, starting every game and playing more minutes than any other U.S. field player.

Lindsey Horan's role on the U.S. team is to serve as its fulcrum: As she slides up and down the pitch, she'll tip the balance from defensive solidity to overwhelming attacking force. . . . Horan is the one who will flip the switch between reasonable caution and ludicrous speed. When she pushes up into the attack, she makes it nigh unstoppable; to cover her and Morgan and Heath and Rapinoe and Lavelle and Dunn and O'Hara in the final third practically requires you to keep ten players back in your own box. . . . She's both the haymaker that can knock opponents out of games and the team's key protection against getting rope-a-doped by someone looking to absorb and counter. Horan can do everything, but on a team this offensively gifted, all she needs to do is everything else.

ERIC BETTS, *Slate*

The 13-0 score line doesn't feel great. Of course it doesn't. But the seven different goal scorers for the U.S. [against Thailand] can't sacrifice their own performance, their team's performance, their mental state going into the next game and the rest of the World Cup because it makes us feel a little gross.

This isn't a new problem for the USWNT—this debate gets brought up time and time again, after they steamroll through lower-ranked countries at CONCACAF qualifiers for the World Cup with double-digit results. But because of the platform of the World Cup, there are more eyeballs on this match than early rounds of regional qualifiers. Some enjoyed the rout, while some immediately brought up sportsmanship.

The U.S. players continued to celebrate goals [in their game against Thailand]. There are definitely some who won't like it, or won't enjoy it, but this wasn't ninety minutes of soccer for them. This was an entire cycle of work come to life. This was the end result of training camps, friendlies, domestic tournaments, domestic club play, individual training for the past four years. This was a celebration of recovering from injuries, earning minutes in a National Team shirt, and every single other moment of hard work.

This wasn't about being nice. It was never about being nice. It is about winning a World Cup.

After the final whistle, the U.S. players immediately went over to the Thai players, shaking hands and telling them to keep their heads up for the next match.

MEG LINEHAN, *The Athletic*

← Critics were quick to condemn the U.S. celebrations during a 13-0 dismantling of Thailand in 2019, but Megan Rapinoe was unapologetic, saying, "That sort of explosion of joy was very genuine for us."

Instead of Team USA being celebrated for what its players achieved, the 13-0 victory over Thailand became an opportunity to lecture these women on how to behave.... True to form, many commentators chided the Americans for gloating.... The ESPN soccer analyst Taylor Twellman weighed in on Twitter: "0.0 problem with the score line as this is THE tournament BUT celebrating goals (like #9) leaves a sour taste in my mouth.... Curious to see if anyone apologizes for this postgame." Well, no one apologized. Nor should anyone have. It isn't the U.S. National Team's job to spare Thailand from humiliation—especially when, in this phase of the tournament, the differential between goals scored and goals allowed can determine whether a team advances. Considering that Alex Morgan tied a tournament record with five goals, and Sam Mewis and Rose Lavelle each scored the first World Cup goals of their careers, this team had every right to celebrate as it wanted.

"You spend your entire life trying to get to a World Cup," wrote Sydney Leroux Dwyer in a text message, "and you get there and you're supposed to tone it down and make people more comfortable?"

JEMELE HILL, *The Atlantic*

→ In the aftermath of the USWNT's onslaught of thirteen goals, Alex Morgan, who scored five of them, consoles the Thai goalkeeper.

The life of Jessica McDonald is littered with losses of control, uncertain pathways, and unpredictable outcomes. Rewards didn't always follow risks, but perseverance did through well-chronicled injuries, motherhood, and a nomadic career. Now, the soccer journey-woman, who recently worked off-season summer jobs to feed her family, is on the verge of spending this summer in France, representing the United States at the Women's World Cup. Few folks, least of all McDonald, would have predicted such a thing mere months ago.

"I'm thirty-one years old, and all the crap that I've been through, the sacrifices, the pushing," says McDonald. "Talk about a dream coming true."

NEIL MORRIS, *The Equalizer*

← Following the USWNT's 2019 World Cup championship, a beaming Jessica McDonald shares the precious trophy with her seven-year-old son, Jeremiah.

↑ Slashing her way through two Chilean defenders during the 2019 World Cup, Mallory Pugh, who joined the team at seventeen, shows why many consider her a future star of the USWNT.

She's never really liked being called a wunderkind, an ephemeral and clichéd description for an athlete who has no intention of being either.

"I feel like it's starting to go away, which I'm very thankful about—the age part," Pugh says. . . . But the future-of-the-sport stuff will likely stick for a while, and it's not just because Pugh was called up to the U-20 National Team at the age of sixteen and went on to become the youngest player for the USWNT to score an Olympic goal, or because she scored fifteen of them by the time she was old enough to drink. Rather, it's because amid all of that she blazed her own path.

After briefly enrolling at UCLA, Pugh decided to forgo NCAA soccer and enter the National Women's Soccer League. . . . By then, she was already heralded as the next big thing. . . . The U.S. Soccer scouts charged with spotting the country's most promising young players developed a detailed plan for her, sort of a how-to manual for assembling the next Mia Hamm. . . . Pugh made her National Team debut in January 2016, scoring off a header against Ireland. That July, Mia Hamm herself tweeted "Speed kills but technical speed absolutely annihilates defenders. Mallory Pugh is for real."

MINA KIMES, *ESPN The Magazine*

Before the opening game of the 2019 World Cup in Reims, France, Megan Rapinoe and Alex Morgan were sitting at their lockers. "One of us has to win the Golden Boot" for the World Cup's top scorer, Rapinoe told her co-captain. But what she really meant was: *You* have to win it. Rapinoe never would have bet on herself to take that award (for which she ultimately edged out Morgan) or the Golden Ball (for MVP) or to be named FIFA's Women's World Player of the Year two months later. "I'm not sure I'm the best player *on my own team*," she admits.

JENNY VRENTAS, *Sports Illustrated*

A free kick by Megan Rapinoe (not pictured) in the opening minutes of the 2019 World Cup quarterfinal slips through a packed box and into the goal, stunning France and propelling the USWNT into the semifinal.

185

Lyon, France—In the 84th minute of a World Cup semifinal, Alyssa Naeher dove to her right and saved a penalty kick off the foot of England's Steph Houghton without allowing a rebound. One England player held her hands on her head in disbelief. Another squeezed the bridge of her nose. Houghton sought stoicism but couldn't suppress a wince.

On the other side of the scale, Americans Alex Morgan and Kelley O'Hara were the first of a swarm of teammates to reach Naeher at full sprint. World Cup winners themselves four years ago, Morgan and O'Hara engulfed her in grateful congratulations as the clock ticked on. Naeher had just preserved a 2-1 lead for the United States.

Without so much as a grin, barely even making eye contact, the goalkeeper pushed them back so she could restart play without risking further sanction from the referee. Not long after, the time ran out and the U.S. was headed back to the final. Naeher has been unheralded and unflappable for three years since taking over from Hope Solo as the No. 1 goalkeeper on the world's top-ranked team. Three years that nonetheless couldn't foretell whether she'd be ready when the career-defining moment arrived. The one moment that might possibly convince people to stop talking about who Naeher isn't and understand who she is.

"I don't think she needed to have a big moment for us to know how good she is," said U.S. captain Becky Sauerbrunn "Maybe for everyone else she needed that moment. But we knew what she was capable of. And now the world knows what she's capable of."

GRAHAM HAYS, *ESPN.com*

Alyssa Naeher makes the save of her life in the 2019 World Cup semifinal against England, stone-walling a penalty kick and preserving a 2-1 U.S. win.

↓ Along with her goal-scoring heroics and outspoken comments, Megan Rapinoe's lilac hair caused a lot of buzz. Future First Lady Jill Biden revealed that she had once dyed her hair the same color in Rapinoe's honor.

Gather your children in front of the flat screen and instruct them to fix their eyes on number 15, the winger with lavender hair. Have them watch as she gallivants down the left flank and flummoxes a defender with a stutter step. Have them listen to her unguarded pregame disquisitions on tactics, Donald Trump, haute couture, and well, every facet of human existence. Tell them that Megan Rapinoe is her generation's Muhammad Ali.

Like her pugilistic forerunner, with whom she shares sly humor and irresistible swagger, the star player on the U.S. Women's National Team has evolved into a hero of resistance. Through her example, Rapinoe has instructed the world on how to play soccer and how to dissent. Her genius is that her political commitments, her public persona, and her playing style are one and the same. In every realm, she is fearlessly open, outrageously joyous, and unabashedly true to herself. . . .

When the tournament bracket thrust the United States into a quarterfinal match with France—a pairing of the two best teams in the world that would have ideally happened in the finals—Rapinoe didn't bemoan the fact, but reveled in it. She told reporters that she wanted a "total shit-show circus" of a spectacle, an occasion from which she intended to extract its full enjoyment, not fear.

FRANKLIN FOER, *The Atlantic*

An abundance of qualities have carried the United States past Spain, France, and now England and into yet another World Cup final, where either the Netherlands or Sweden awaits on Sunday. The finishing of Morgan—scorer of what proved the decisive goal here on Tuesday—is one of them.

So, too, in no particular order: the dynamism of Crystal Dunn; the mesmerizing dribbling of Tobin Heath; the ingenuity of Megan Rapinoe and the explosiveness of her replacement, Christen Press; the strength of Julie Ertz; Lindsey Horan's ability, in Morgan's words, to "play any pass"; and the joyful, inventive brilliance of Rose Lavelle, by some distance the best player on the field in this semifinal.

More important still than the individual characteristics, though, are the collective ones. This United States team has a self-confidence that has set as concrete; it is not so much that it seems to go into every game expecting to win, but that it appears not to have heard about the possibility of defeat. It is keenly aware of the legacy it has inherited, the standards it is expected to keep, the glories that have gone before, and it does not shy from them. Instead, it embraces the challenge, the chance to prove itself worthy of the torch inherited from Mia Hamm and Brandi Chastain and the rest. . . .

They do not see themselves as the standard-bearers for some idea of how the game should be played or what it should look like. It would be wrong to say there is no aesthetic quality to what they do; more that they accept that aesthetics are subjective—what looks beautiful to some may be dull to others—and that their concern is, primarily, with the objective.

This is a team built to win: whenever, wherever, and however that might be. . . . That is all that matters—that, to this incarnation of women's soccer's greatest dynasty, is all that there is.

RORY SMITH, *New York Times*

On July 2, 2019—her thirtieth birthday—Alex Morgan receives a gift-wrapped cross from Lindsey Horan that she takes in full stride, planting a header in the corner of the England net.

There is some sort of double standard for females in sport to feel like we have to be humble in our successes and have to celebrate but not too much. You see men celebrate all over the world in big tournaments, you know, grabbing their sacks or whatever it is.

—

ALEX MORGAN, *2019 World Cup press conference before final*

→
Morgan's "sip of tea" goal celebration outraged much of England, but she shrugged off the critics as if they were so many Lioness defenders.

Four years after sitting in a pizza shop and watching Carli Lloyd lead the American women to the 2015 World Cup championship, Rose Lavelle scores a wonder goal to clinch the 2019 title and etch her name in USWNT history.

Rose Lavelle was nine and a half—the half is important, if you're nine—when the women that changed everything arrived in Cincinnati.

It was October 2004, a few months after the United States women's soccer team had won the gold medal in the Athens Olympics, five years after it had conquered the world. Mia Hamm, Brandi Chastain, and the rest were traveling the country, playing exhibition games, as a sort of victory tour.

Lavelle was there to watch at the Paul Brown Stadium for a game against New Zealand. It was more of a carnival than a contest: The Americans won, 6-0, the sort of procession that—in the eyes of a child—befitted their greatness. Lavelle fell for them, and fell hard.

She became "obsessed," she said a few weeks ago, with the team that would go down in history as the 99ers, the team that won the World Cup on home soil in the year that became its calling card, the team that transformed the arc of women's soccer in the United States and, more slowly, around the globe.

. . . On Sunday, in the baking heat of Lyon, Lavelle scored the second, clinching goal as the latest incarnation of the United States Women's National Team beat the Netherlands, 2-0, not just to lift the World Cup, but to do what the 99ers did not quite manage, and retain it. "It's crazy how things come full circle," Lavelle said. . . .

Just as the young Lavelle watched, rapt, as Hamm and Chastain and the rest swept past New Zealand, transfixed by their greatness, so too will aspirant internationals watch Lavelle with shining eyes; just as the young [Lindsey] Horan pored over videos of that Olympic triumph in Athens, so too will the clips and gifs of what she and her teammates have achieved hypnotize a new generation. "Hopefully we will become legends to future internationals," she said.

. . . High in the stands of the Stade de Lyon, two girls stood watching the United States celebrate, glitter spread across the field, firework smoke in the air. They looked about eight or nine. Heath and Horan, their jerseys read. They looked down at the celebrations. They stood perfectly still. They could not tear their eyes away.

RORY SMITH, *New York Times*

If anything, calling this year's USWNT the greatest American soccer team of all time feels like selling them short. They faced unprecedentedly strong opposition, and they ground that opposition into ash.

Along the way, of course, they were the targets of petty criticism from a whole host of detractors, ranging from their opponents to the international media to people looking for reasons to hate women's soccer to the president of the United States. They were attacked for scoring too many goals and also for being overconfident. They were attacked for celebrating too jubilantly and also for being too angrily political. They were attacked—possibly by their own parents—for having once, several months ago, used the word "f-ing." They were attacked for being un-American and also for performing perhaps the single most patriotic action available to any citizen of this country: trolling England in a manner involving tea.

BRIAN PHILLIPS, *The Ringer*

2020

EACH NEW
GENERATION MUST
ANSWER THE
QUESTION:
WHO WILL COME
UP CLUTCH
WHEN THE STAKES
ARE HIGHEST?

→
Against Australia in 2021, Lindsey
Horan wears the captain's armband
for the USWNT, which is counting
on U.S. Soccer's Player of the Year
to take the team to new heights.

BIG SHOES TO FILL

BY **GWENDOLYN OXENHAM**

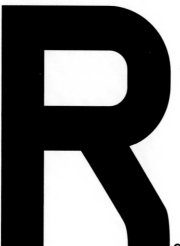

ROSE LAVELLE and Carli Lloyd are riding a crowded elevator in a hotel in Frisco, Texas. It's 2018 and Lloyd, unknowingly, is standing atop the tips of Lavelle's sandals. If an ordinary person were stepping on her, Lavelle might've said excuse me or inched backward. But Carli Lloyd is not an ordinary person. Carli Lloyd scored a hat trick in a sixteen-minute stretch to win the 2015 World Cup for the U.S. Not to mention her Olympic-winning goals in 2008 and 2012. This is the person who has lived Lavelle's wildest dreams. So no, she doesn't say a word. But she does covertly record this moment with her phone—the time when a superhero stood on her feet.

Three years later, on October 26, 2021, the day thirty-nine-year-old Carli retires, Lavelle posts the video in Lloyd's honor. She explains that day in the elevator, how she "was too nervous to say anything." To close, she adds, "Thank you Carli." Thank you, Carli, for showing us what's possible.

Showing why she's one of the bright hopes for the future of the USWNT, Catarina Macario dusts a Colombian defender in a 2021 match.

This generation has glamorous Instagram pages and social-media savvy. They have spent less time in the shadows, more time in the spotlight.

The generation that has dazzled the world, winning back-to-back World Cups and three Olympic gold medals in a row, will soon fade out. At the 2020 Olympics, where the U.S. finishes a disappointing third, ten of the eighteen U.S. players are past their thirtieth birthday, but a vibrant infusion of youth is on the way.

The coming transition will test everyone. And Lavelle, you could say, has a tangible understanding: These are big shoes to fill.

THIRTY-SEVEN YEARS AGO, in the coastal town of Jesolo, Italy, the very first U.S. Women's National Team took the field in passed-down men's jerseys—women's cut jerseys did not yet exist. They were new kids on the scene and had played together for less than a week. They went home winless after four games. But they were better than their results indicated. They had a certain renegade spirit. They often played on guys' teams or traveled long distances in search of others who loved the game like they did.

But Title IX slowly changed things. With every passing year, more schools implemented the landmark legislation, which required men's and women's programs to have equal funding. This created more school teams and more college scholarships.

↑ The "likes" keep mounting as USWNT stars like Alex Morgan (above) blow up on social media. Lifelong friends Jaelin Howell and Sophia Smith (above right) were on the same team as seven-year-olds.

← One generation pays homage to another as Carli Lloyd and Rose Lavelle salute each other following the USWNT victory over Paraguay in 2021.

Those USWNT pioneers forged their own path, though, sewing on U.S. patches, explaining to their parents what a World Cup was, and passing out flyers themselves.

AND THEN, in 1999, more than 90,000 fans filled the Rose Bowl to watch the United States win the World Cup in a penalty shootout—and every generation thereafter has grown up knowing exactly what the dream could look like. Megan Rapinoe and Christen Press had been kids in the stands. Rose Lavelle dressed up as Mia Hamm for a third-grade book report, homemade gold medal hanging from her neck. Catarina Macario wasn't born yet—but years later, in Brasilia, while watching YouTube videos of Mia Hamm, Macario and her father were intrigued by the idea of playing in the United States. Meanwhile, in California, Sophia Smith and *her* father were entranced by YouTube videos of Brazilian star Marta. "Everyone talks about how important it is to be able to see people doing what you dream of doing," says Smith, "and that's exactly what happened with me."

The "see-it-to-dream-it" effect—and Title IX—have created a country of girls who want to be great. Today over a million young girls play soccer in the States. Little enclaves of talent pop up here and there: USWNT players Lindsey Horan, Mallory Pugh, Sophia Smith, and Jaelin Howell all hail from the suburbs around Denver; incredibly, Smith and Howell were on the same kindergarten team. And there seems to be something in the drinking water in Dallas, Texas, where the Solar Soccer Club put *seven* kids in the 2022 U-15 National Team pool. There are youth national teams for every age group beginning at thirteen; some

30,000 girls go on to play soccer in college. In the increasingly robust U.S. pro league, the NWSL, approximately 312 women are being paid to play soccer. The more the game grows, the harder it becomes to land a spot on the National Team.

THE CURRENT GENERATION has glamorous Instagram pages and social-media savvy. They have spent less time in the shadows, more time in the spotlight; often mic'ed up at practice, we can hear every breath, every snatch of banter. Players wear sleek, well-cut training gear and high-tech monitors that track each step, each heartbeat. Several National Team players have endorsements, commercials, and seven-figure incomes. At the club level, starting NWSL salaries are now $35,000 plus benefits, five times what they were when the league was founded in 2012. Today's National Team now travels on chartered flights to world-class facilities—a far cry from the

Always seeking to challenge themselves at the highest level, Catarina Macario (left) and Lindsey Horan team up to help Europe's storied dynasty Olympic Lyonnais defeat Barcelona 3-1 in the 2022 Champions League final in which Macario scores a goal.

early days of coal trains in China and gravel practice fields in Italy. Yet that doesn't mean they've gone soft: Making the 2023 World Cup team—fighting your way through the thicket of talent—requires more toughness than ever before.

The 2023 World Cup roster has not yet been finalized, but the players vying for a spot on the U.S. team share that trademark hunger—the *need* to be great.

CONSIDER Lindsay Horan, who skipped playing girls high school soccer and instead played spring ball with the guys, since she knew that would make her better. Then, famously, she spurned college and went straight to the pros, even though no American woman had ever done that before. At eighteen, she signed with one of Europe's top clubs, Paris Saint-Germain (PSG), because she believed it was the fastest route to realizing her dreams. She knew there were people who thought she was making a mistake. "Everyone says you grow into who you are in college," says Horan. "I wondered if I would still grow into who I am if I didn't go to college. I thought, *I'll find a different way to grow*."

First minutes in France, still at the airport: Horan got her untied shoelaces stuck in the escalator. She caused a pileup, people shouting at her in French, her mother laughing at her in the background. Can anything make you feel more like a child than getting your shoelaces stuck in an escalator? Was it a sign?

"One of the main reasons I made the choice I did was to be uncomfortable," Horan says. "I wanted to risk everything to make the National Team." Ultimately, she scored forty-six goals in fifty-eight games with PSG.

But she was not chosen for the 2015 World Cup team. "I remember sitting in the stands as a fan in Canada and thinking, *I hate this right now*," says Horan. "It hit me—I needed to be better. That was *the* moment that really changed things."

In 2016, she headed back to the States to play for the Portland Thorns. In the 2017 league final, she scored the only goal and was selected as the game's MVP. And by the 2019 World Cup, you can bet she wasn't watching from the stands; in game one, she started in the U.S. midfield alongside fellow newcomers Samantha Mewis and Rose Lavelle.

Horan blazed a new path—and others have followed. Teenage sensations Trinity Rodman and Mal Pugh also skipped college soccer and went straight to the pros. Catarina Macario and Sophia Smith left Stanford early.

↑ Sofia Huerta, one of only two women ever to play both for Mexico and the USWNT, is among the players shaping the future of the team.

The 2023 World Cup roster has not yet been finalized, but the players vying for a spot on the U.S. team share that trademark hunger—the *need* to be great.

As with Smith, awed whispers followed Macario ("She's special, she's the future."). Playing together for Stanford, they won a national championship.

↓ Andi Sullivan (left) and Kelley O'Hara (center) helped drive their club team, the Washington Spirit, to the 2021 NWSL championship.

SMITH BEGAN competing on youth national teams when she was twelve, playing one age division up. At fifteen, she was selected for the under seventeen World Cup team in Jordan. She remembers the brown buildings, the toll of the bells, and—most vividly—sitting on the bench. "My role was minimal," she says flatly.

Her club coach, former Jamaican national team player Lorne Donaldson, recalled the time *he* tried to bench her. Smith had scored seven goals in the first half; her team was up 10-0. "Sophie, you're done," he told her. She balked.

He explained that he didn't want to embarrass the other coach.

Donaldson still remembers what she said next: "That's not *my* problem—that's *his* problem. I came to play."

Smith lives to score. There is no cap on goals, no "enough"—she will score and score again. After the U-17 World Cup in Jordan? "I wanted to prove everyone wrong," she says. She scored nine goals in the next six games, a youth national team record.

Her Bambi eyes are deceptive—*she's* the one going for the kill. She very much looks like she's on the hunt: Her run is smooth, fierce, calculating. The kid who binged Marta YouTube videos is fond of tricks—but she doesn't use them idly. She nutmegs you because it's the fastest route to goal.

In 2018, Smith began her first year at Stanford. There she played alongside Catarina Macario, who had made it all the way to Palo Alto from São Luis, Brazil. Macario grew up playing barefoot in a narrow street with the neighborhood boys, using pairs of stray bricks or Havaianas flip-flops to mark goals, pausing the game for passing cars. "It was a thrill," says Macario. She was the girl playing with grown men at her uncle's ranch; she was the girl playing futsal on the courts and *futevolei* (soccer volleyball) on the beaches. "It's like dancing," she says, and she credits Brazil with giving her "that bit of *ginga*," a Portuguese word for that special blend of flair and imagination.

When Macario was twelve and no longer allowed to play with the boys' teams in Brazil, her father sent an email to an American club coach, Chris Lemay: "My daughter is interested in playing soccer in America and we're coming for a visit." Lemay, accustomed to such quixotic messages—which almost never led to anything—shot off a quick "sure, come by." Several weeks later, Macario showed up on the field in San Diego. When Lemay got home that night, he told his wife: Macario was the best player he'd ever witnessed.

As with Smith, awed whispers followed Macario ("She's special, she's the future."). Playing together for Stanford, they won a national championship.

Title checked off, each moved on from Palo Alto—Macario to the European juggernaut Olympique Lyonnais, and Smith to the Portland Thorns. The two of them understand that dominating at the college level is different from dominating in the pros, and they are itching to take their place in the Darwinian competition for one of the coveted twenty-three World Cup roster spots.

To do that, they will have to prove themselves against other young players, such as Trinity Rodman, Andi Sullivan, Ashley Hatch, and Ashley Sanchez, all of

whom excelled for the 2021 NWSL champions, the Washington Spirit, and have been invited to National Team camps by coach Vlatko Andonovski as he builds his final roster before the 2023 World Cup.

The level these young players must reach is extraordinarily high. For one thing, the veterans *know* each other—which you can see in their silky combination play and intuitive understanding of space and each other.

ULTIMATELY, the quality that defines the stars of the U.S. team is the ability to score in big-time games against the best. Like when Megan Rapinoe sent a wonder-cross to the head of Abby Wambach in the dying seconds of the 2011 World Cup quarterfinal; or when Carli Lloyd scored in the 2008 and 2012 Olympic finals; or when Alex Morgan scored an impossible header in stoppage time at the end of extra time—in the 123rd minute!—to beat Canada in the 2012 Olympic semifinals. Or in the 69th minute of the 2019 World Cup final against the Netherlands, when Rose Lavelle tore up the field, cut left, and buried the ball inside the right post—and straight into USWNT folklore.

↑ On her way to the USWNT roster, Sophia Smith stopped off at Stanford, helping the Cardinal win a national championship in 2019.

↓ Known for his meticulous preparation and tactical flexibility, Vlatko Andonovski has reenergized the USWNT by bringing in a new generation of talented players.

Horan has a sweeping, Houdini-like presence, unlocking closed defenses . . . pulling the game toward her like she is tidal and all-powerful.

Lavelle is five-foot-four and skinny. She has heard more than once that she is too tiny, too slight. "That kind of rejection motivated me. I was out for revenge, to show what they'd missed out on," says Lavelle. "If you think that, the joke's on you." She has become technical—remarkably technical—so she can create separation: "then they can't buck me off the ball." Lavelle's small size works in her favor—she is *more* evasive, like a leprechaun who dances and tricks and disappears, too quick to catch.

Off the field, she is also wily, playful, and impish.

Once, when Lavelle and Horan were roommates on a road trip, Lavelle snuck onto Horan's open Twitter account and, pretending to be Horan, conducted a poll: What should my nickname be? Lavelle posted multiple options, including the Great Horan. "People are voting—she's off giggling, and I have no idea what she's giggling about," says Horan. The votes came in steadily—the Great Horan was the clear winner—and Lindsey was mortified that people might think she was cocky enough to nickname herself that. But the moniker is apt: She has a sweeping, Houdini-like presence, unlocking closed defenses, materializing in space, pulling the game toward her, like she is tidal and all-powerful. Her transatlantic journey appears to have been worth it: She was named U.S. Soccer's Female Player of the Year in 2021.

That same year, she began wearing the iconic number 10 jersey, made famous by the likes of Pelé and Messi, Michelle Akers and Carli Lloyd—and now Horan.

The Great Horan—Lavelle, of course, coined the nickname in jest because she knew her modest friend would hate it. But make no mistake, greatness is what they're all after. It's more than just a place on the National Team and a plane ticket to Australia and New Zealand in June 2023. Greatness means living up to the standard of excellence created by those who have come before you—filling those big shoes and going beyond.

←
The number 10 has been worn by the greatest players in the history of the game and carries prestige that's unique among soccer jerseys. Upon Carli Lloyd's retirement following her epic USWNT career, Lindsey Horan became the next player to rock the hallowed shirt.

GUARDIANS OF THE CREST

Their task? Something no team has ever done before: Win a third straight World Cup. On the following pages, meet the players who are competing for the honor of representing the USWNT at the 2023 World Cup in Australia and New Zealand. They are a mix of veterans who won the 2015 and 2019 World Cups and emerging young stars, some of whom are barely out of college. Together they will try adding a fifth star to the American crest.

FIFA World Cup
Experience:
2019

Position:
Midfielder

Nickname:
Rosie

Height: **5'4"**

Birthdate:
May 14, 1995

Hometown:
Cincinnati, OH

College:
**University of
Wisconsin**

First USWNT Cap:
March 4, 2017

Notable Honors:
**2021 SheBelieves Cup
MVP, 2019 FIFA World
Cup Bronze Ball, 2014
CONCACAF Women's
U-20 Championship
Golden Ball, four-time
All-Big Ten First Team**

FYI:
**Her English bulldog,
Wilma Jean Wrinkles,
has nearly 14,000
Instagram followers**

Instagram:
lavellerose

Twitter:
@roselavelle

ROSE
LAVELLE

YOU THINK YOU'VE TRAPPED HER in a tight corner with nowhere to go but Rose Lavelle has other ideas. A step-over here, a pirouette there, a nutmeg everywhere. You don't know what to expect and, suddenly, she's dancing free in the open field. Lunge at the ball and she will pull it back or cut it so sharply you are tackling nothing but air. She is a five-foot-four twirling nightmare of tricks and flicks. Now her legs are whirring and you are in retreat and looking for help. Maybe she will thread a perfectly weighted pass through a sliver of space and onto a teammate's foot. Or maybe she will just keep coming at you, accelerating with every stride, caressing the ball with small, delicate touches. Her head is up, her eyes calculating every possibility. Suddenly she is at the top of the box, dropping her shoulder and shifting the ball to her left foot. Watch her shoot, unleashing a precision-guided missile beyond the goalkeeper's reach. Now watch Rose Lavelle score.

↑ With crafty moves and electric bursts, Lavelle keeps defenders off-balance, as she does here against Mexico in 2021.

LINDSEY

YOU WANT TO LIVE DANGEROUSLY? Try getting past the force of nature known as Lindsey Horan. You'll be met by a harrying whirlwind who will dispossess you, beat you off the dribble, and barrel into the box oblivious to the riot of opponents' sharp elbows and rock-hard knees. The 2021 U.S. Soccer Female Player of the Year, Horan is a triple threat: disrupter, orchestrator, assassin. She always turns up where the team needs her to be. It's almost as if she has a tracking device in her brain that guides her movements. There's no one who can outduel her for the ball. No one who can bisect the defense better with a scalpel-sharp pass from midfield. No one with her tensile strength. When she thumps a header, the net feels it.

HORAN

↑ With exquisite timing, Horan thunders into the box to whistle a shot into the back of the net against Mexico in 2021.

FIFA World Cup
Experience:
2019

Position:
Midfielder

Nickname:
The Great Horan

Height: **5'9"**

Birthdate:
May 26, 1994

Hometown:
Golden, CO

First USWNT Cap:
March 8, 2013

Notable Honors:
**2018 NWSL MVP,
2021 U.S. Soccer
Female Player of
the Year**

FYI:
**Has a French
bulldog named
Ferguson, "Fergs"
for short**

Instagram:
lindseyhoran10

Twitter:
@LindseyHoran

FIFA World Cup Experience:
2019

Position:
Midfielder

Nickname:
Tower of Power

Height: **6'0"**

Birthdate:
October 9, 1992

Hometown:
Hanson, MA

College:
UCLA

First USWNT Cap:
March 7, 2014

Notable Honors:
2020 U.S. Soccer Female Player of the Year, 2017 NWSL Best XI

FYI:
To celebrate making the 2020 Olympic team, Sam and her sister, Kristie, created their own special-edition beer, the Mew-S-A Citrus IPA

Instagram:
sammymewyy

Twitter:
@sammymewy

SAMANTHA MEWIS

YOU THINK SHE DOESN'T SEE YOU as you're about to swoop in, but she has already shifted the ball from one foot to the other, a simple but assured touch that leaves you flailing helplessly. And now she's sprinting upfield, eating up space with her long-legged strides. The tallest field player in USWNT history at six feet, she looms over the landscape, nothing escaping her vision. Samantha Mewis is the epitome of the driving, passing, scoring midfielder who can seize the game in any number of ways. Will she deploy that howitzer of a right foot from outside the box before the goalkeeper can move a muscle? Or will it be a defense-cleaving through-ball that shreds the opponent? Or does she wait for a high, arcing cross in the goalmouth, where she skies, head and shoulders above the rest, to nod it home? It could be any or all of them.

Just call her the Tower of Power.

↑ Blessed with a ferocious right foot, Mewis can launch rockets from distance. Here she takes aim in the bronze medal match against Australia at the 2020 Olympics.

CRYSTAL

SHE IS BOMBING DOWN the flank in a blur while her opponents are furiously back-pedaling. With a shimmy of the hips or a turn-on-a-dime cutback, she surges to the end line to deliver a cross or marauds through the midfield to slip a teammate through on goal. Or she hurtles in from behind with a perfectly timed sliding tackle as an opponent breaks on the counter, foolishly thinking she's home free. Thanks to her unmatched versatility, you will find Crystal Dunn everywhere. Just a headband over five feet with a low center of gravity and muscular legs that catapult her over opponents a half-foot taller, she's morphed from a menacing goal-scoring threat into a lockdown defender given license to roam. In the process, she has weaponized the position of left back on the USWNT. "As a defender, I can anticipate what a forward will do because I've been one," she says. "And vice versa."

Pity the opponent who has to play both Crystal Dunns at once.

DUNN

↑ Whether disrupting attacks or flying up the field with the ball at her feet, the versatile Dunn was equally dangerous against England at the SheBelieves Cup in 2020.

FIFA World Cup
Experience:
2019

Position:
Defender

Nickname:
Dunny

Height: **5'2"**

Birthdate:
July 3, 1992

Hometown:
Rockville Centre, NY

College:
**University of North
Carolina**

First USWNT Cap:
February 13, 2013

Notable Honors:
**2018 CONCACAF
Women's Best XI,
2015 NWSL Golden
Boot, 2015 NWSL
MVP**

FYI:
**Unofficial DJ in
locker room and
best dancer on
the team**

Instagram:
cdunn19

Twitter:
@Cdunn19

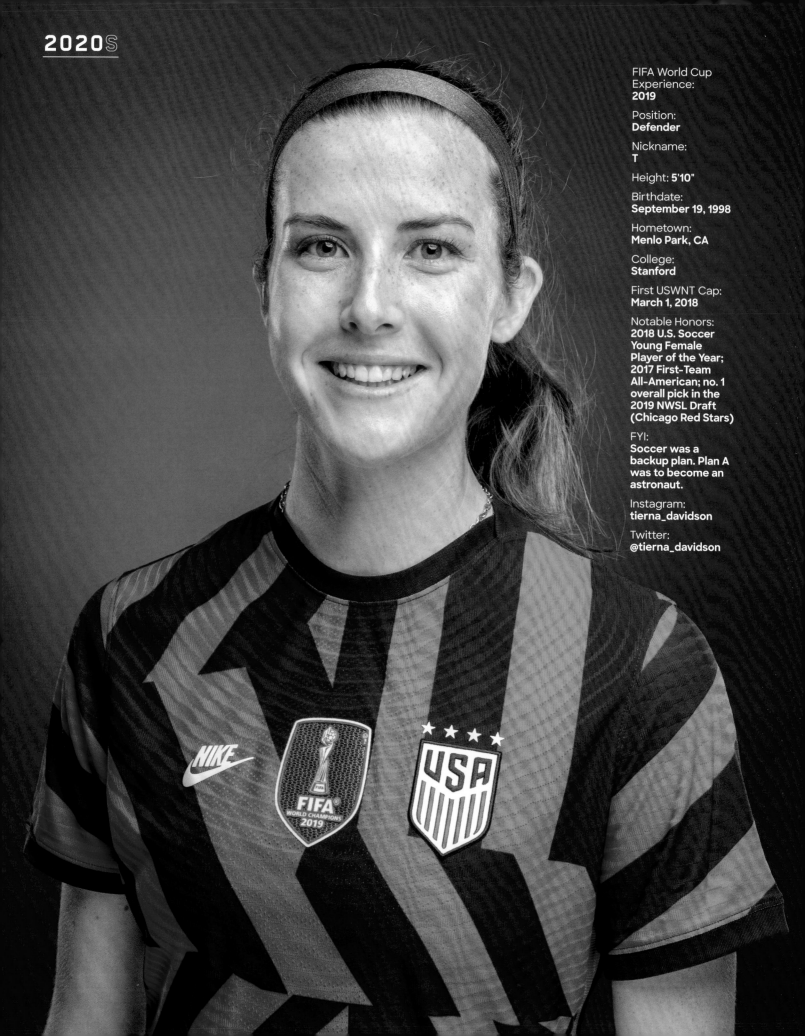

FIFA World Cup
Experience:
2019

Position:
Defender

Nickname:
T

Height: **5'10"**

Birthdate:
September 19, 1998

Hometown:
Menlo Park, CA

College:
Stanford

First USWNT Cap:
March 1, 2018

Notable Honors:
**2018 U.S. Soccer
Young Female
Player of the Year;
2017 First-Team
All-American; no. 1
overall pick in the
2019 NWSL Draft
(Chicago Red Stars)**

FYI:
**Soccer was a
backup plan. Plan A
was to become an
astronaut.**

Instagram:
tierna_davidson

Twitter:
@tierna_davidson

TIERNA DAVIDSON

Davidson rarely betrays nerves on either side of the ball. "I guess I look composed at all times," she says. "That calm has always been with me from an early age."

THE PASS is just a little short, a little slow. And by the time she collects it along the sideline, two opponents dive bomb her from either side. She's trapped with no place to go. Does Tierna Davidson panic? Does she even for a moment appear rattled? Cool as you like, she splits them with a quicksilver dribble and a razor-edged pass that slices apart the high press. This is her greatest gift—her ability to play out of pressure and to look so relaxed doing it you'd never know there was a high-stakes game going on. At twenty, she has the battle-hardened unflappability of a veteran center-back. She knows when to step or drop, to pick the right moment to assert her presence. And with a left foot that is surgical in its accuracy, her free kicks and corners pose a threat every time instep meets ball. Her mentor and fellow center-back Becky Sauerbrunn has no doubt: "Tierna is going to be the best defender in the world."

ALEX MORGAN

IT STARTS ON TIPPY-TOES and ends with a billowing net. Those are the twin pillars of an Alex Morgan goal—more than a hundred of them in international soccer and counting. She's a bolt of attacking menace. She rises to thump a spring-loaded header. She gallops hell-bent to beat her defender to a through-ball. She unleashes a game-winning strike with a fearsome left foot worthy of Abby Wambach or Kristine Lilly. You want to win a bet? Ask someone how many matches the USWNT has lost when Morgan has scored a goal. Answer (as of early 2022): None.

As remarkable as that statistic is, it doesn't tell the full story of her skill set. In addition to her dead-eye finishes, there's the subtle movement off the ball that creates space for her teammates; the slick passing that carves apart a defense; the ability to use her weaker right foot to score: Wherever, however, forever, Alex Morgan is a threat.

↑ No matter how many defenders try to stop her, if you allow Morgan a sliver of space and let her put her left foot through the ball, you're in trouble.

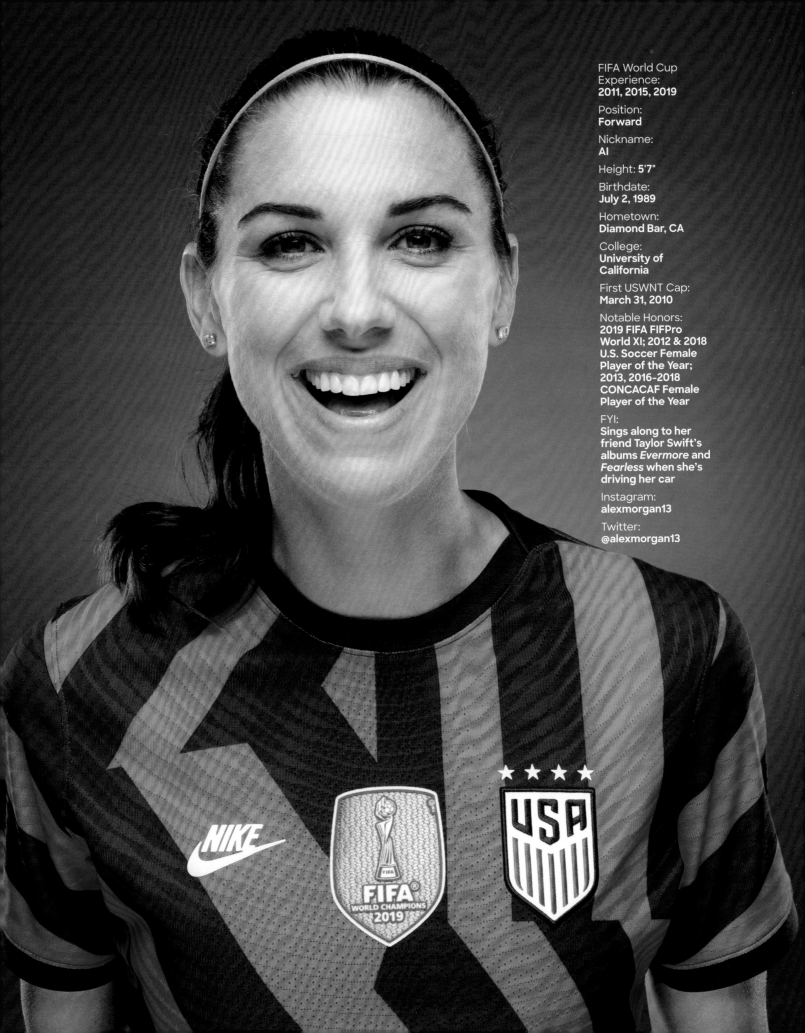

FIFA World Cup
Experience:
2011, 2015, 2019

Position:
Forward

Nickname:
AI

Height: **5'7"**

Birthdate:
July 2, 1989

Hometown:
Diamond Bar, CA

College:
**University of
California**

First USWNT Cap:
March 31, 2010

Notable Honors:
**2019 FIFA FIFPro
World XI; 2012 & 2018
U.S. Soccer Female
Player of the Year;
2013, 2016–2018
CONCACAF Female
Player of the Year**

FYI:
**Sings along to her
friend Taylor Swift's
albums *Evermore* and
Fearless when she's
driving her car**

Instagram:
alexmorgan13

Twitter:
@alexmorgan13

FIFA World Cup
Experience:
2015, 2019

Position:
Forward

Nickname:
CP

Height: **5'7"**

Birthdate:
December 29, 1988

Hometown:
**Palos Verdes
Estates, CA**

College:
Stanford

First USWNT Cap:
February 9, 2013

Notable Honors:
**2015-17, 2019 NWSL
Best XI; Starting XI on
Pac-12 All-Century
Team; 2010 Hermann
Trophy**

FYI:
**Serves as CEO of an
eco-friendly global
lifestyle company
called re—inc that
she started in 2019
with teammates
Megan Rapinoe,
Tobin Heath, and
Meghan Klingenberg**

Instagram:
christenpress

Twitter:
@ChristenPress

CHRISTEN PRESS

IF THERE WERE A MUSEUM for artful goals, Christen Press would have her own wing. Thunderbolt from outside the eighteen? Check. Bending balls that shave the post? Check. Delicate lobs over an outfoxed keeper? Check. Fast-twitch flicks in the goalmouth? Check.

In other words, once she gets the ball in a dangerous area, you'll likely be picking it out of the net seconds later. What makes her so deadly is not just her speed afoot but her speed of thought. Decisions are made without breaking stride and with a minimum of touches. Everything is done with an understated flair but with the cunning of a safe cracker. Her strikes are pure and clean, launched off whichever foot she chooses. The opposing goalkeeper might as well be checking her cellphone.

↑ Compact, balanced, and with ruthless intent, Press dribbles past an opponent into the heart of the Portugal defense during a 2021 match.

PRESS

TOBIN HEATH

← No one on the U.S. Team plays with more cheeky exuberance than Heath, shown here beating a Dutch defender in the 2020 Olympics.

SEEING TOBIN HEATH'S off-the-cuff genius with the ball, you might think she grew up on the beaches of Brazil instead of in the suburbs of New Jersey. Such is her improvisational wizardry that even her teammates marvel when she pulls off yet another face-melting trick—shimmies, step-overs, back-heels, nutmegs—and have we mentioned her signature elastico, a dizzying, ankle-breaking double feint that leaves defenders sprawled on the turf? She's so unpredictable that she herself doesn't know what her next move will be. All she knows is that there's an opponent standing in her path, and one way or another, she's going to rinse her—and entertain us while doing it. Therein lies the joy of the game for Tobin Heath and the jaw-dropping wonder for the rest of us.

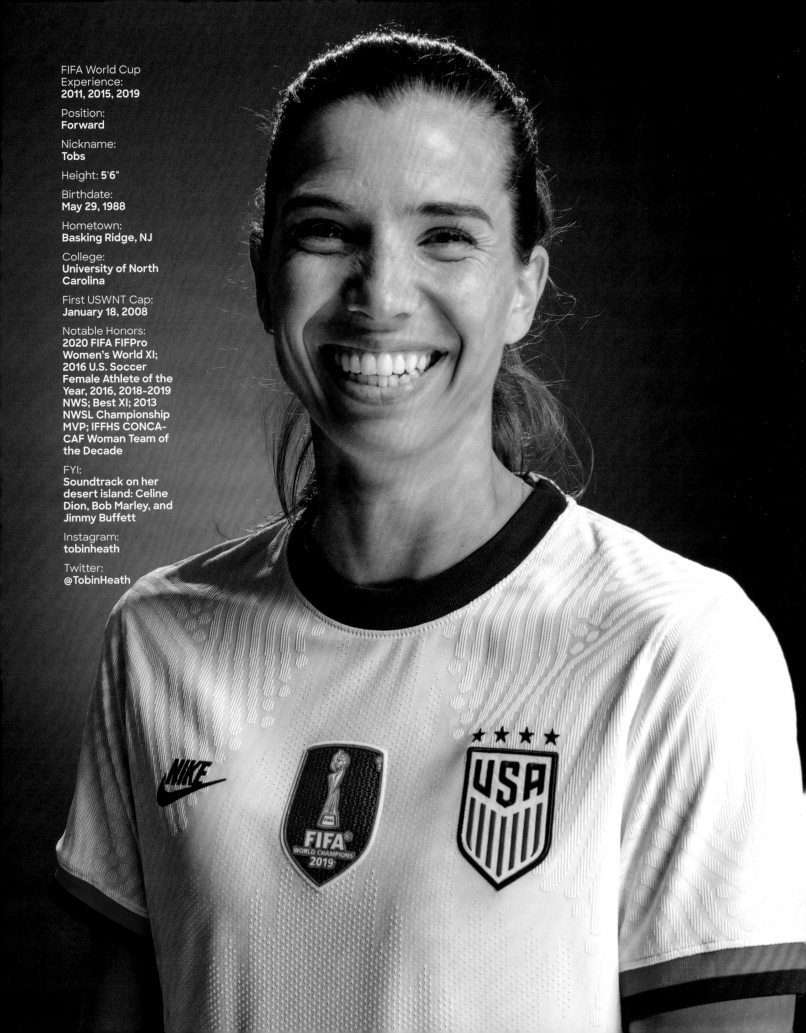

FIFA World Cup
Experience:
2011, 2015, 2019

Position:
Forward

Nickname:
Tobs

Height: **5'6"**

Birthdate:
May 29, 1988

Hometown:
Basking Ridge, NJ

College:
**University of North
Carolina**

First USWNT Cap:
January 18, 2008

Notable Honors:
**2020 FIFA FIFPro
Women's World XI;
2016 U.S. Soccer
Female Athlete of the
Year, 2016, 2018-2019
NWS; Best XI; 2013
NWSL Championship
MVP; IFFHS CONCA-
CAF Woman Team of
the Decade**

FYI:
**Soundtrack on her
desert island: Celine
Dion, Bob Marley, and
Jimmy Buffett**

Instagram:
tobinheath

Twitter:
@TobinHeath

FIFA World Cup
Experience:
None

Position:
Midfielder

Nickname:
Cat

Height: **5'5"**

Birthdate:
October 4, 1999

Hometown:
San Diego, CA

College:
Stanford

First USWNT Cap:
January 18, 2021

Notable Honors:
**2018-19 MAC
Hermann Trophy
winner; 2017 Pac-12
Freshman of the Year**

FYI:
**On October 9, 2020,
she became a U.S.
citizen and within
hours she was invited
to her first USWNT
training camp.**

Instagram:
catarina_macario

Twitter:
@catarinamacario

CATARINA MACARIO

ONE-HUNDRED-FIFTY seconds. That's all it took for Catarina Macario to score in her first start for the USWNT. That's all it took for her to serve notice that she may be the future of the National Team: 150 seconds.

Seldom has a player arrived with greater anticipation than this electrifying Brazilian-born, Stanford-educated dynamo. Blessed with outrageous skills, uncanny vision, and poise beyond her years, she makes the impossible happen. Watch her kill a ball on her thigh, flick it up in the air, and volley it with effortless technique into the top corner; watch her knife through a packed defense, all power and athleticism, to spank a shot past a helpless goalkeeper; watch her shoot fiercely on the turn from the top of the box; watch her bending, swerving, rocketing free kicks into the upper ninety. And she does all this with the flair and exuberance of a player just beginning to explore the infinite possibilities of her talent.

↑ Swift as she is smooth, Macario slips a pass through the legs of a Paraguayan defender during a 2021 match in which she scored two goals.

225

MALLORY PUGH

← The Thai goalkeeper comes up empty as the quicksilver Pugh whooshes past her while scoring a goal in the USWNT's 2019 World Cup opener.

SHE IS HEADING YOUR WAY. Cherubic face, diminutive stature. . . . Nothing to worry about, right? Except she's in full flight, and you're about to be left in her slipstream. You can dive in for a tackle and swipe at the air, or back up and wait for help to arrive. Either way, you're in a world of hurt. Pugh has the kind of close control at searing pace that makes defenders wish they had missed the team bus. Without breaking stride, she can change direction in a microsecond, twisting you this way and that. But she can do a lot more than simply dribble you senseless. Her passing is tidy, her movements off the ball clever, her finishing deadly.

And suddenly you realize that her angelic looks disguise the face of a ruthless sniper.

FIFA World Cup
Experience:
2019

Position:
Forward

Nickname:
Mal

Height: **5'4"**

Birthdate:
April 29, 1998

Hometown:
Highlands Ranch, CO

College:
UCLA

First USWNT Cap:
January 23, 2016

Notable Honors:
2016 Gatorade National Female Soccer Player of the Year; 2015 U.S. Soccer Young Female Player of the Year

FYI:
Knows all the lyrics to "Jumpman" by rappers Drake and Future

Instagram:
malpugh

Twitter:
@MalPugh

FIFA World Cup
Experience:
2019

Position:
Defender

Nickname:
Saucy Sonny

Height: **5'7"**

Birthdate:
November 25, 1993

Hometown:
Marietta, GA

College:
University of Virginia

First USWNT Cap:
October 25, 2015

Notable Honors:
**2018 NWSL Best XI;
2015 NSCAA First-
Team All-American**

FYI:
**That person eating
banana pancakes
at your local Waffle
House might actually
be Emily Sonnett**

Instagram:
emilysonnett

Twitter:
@emilysonnett

EMILY SONNETT

↑ Known for her take-no-prisoners defending, Sonnett can be equally dogged when driving down the field.

THE SCOWL you see on the field is named Emily Sonnett. Yapping at the refs. Scything down opponents. Challenging her teammates to match her vein-popping intensity. That smile you see off the field is also named Emily Sonnett. Her antic personality keeps the team loose, but once the whistle blows, the impish grin falls away and there's nothing funny about her game. Feisty, pugnacious, and tireless, she's the kind of versatile baller every coach needs—someone who can do the dirty work wherever it's required. In midfield. In central defense. Or as an outside back who can play on either flank and use her speed and tenacity to clamp down on dangerous attackers. Every team needs a dose of Emily Sonnett.

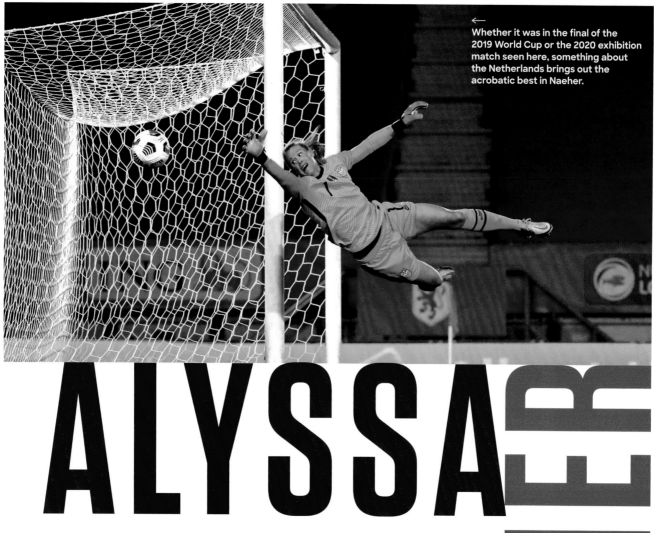

Whether it was in the final of the 2019 World Cup or the 2020 exhibition match seen here, something about the Netherlands brings out the acrobatic best in Naeher.

ALYSSA NAEHER

IS THERE A LONELIER PLACE on the planet than the patch of ground between those two posts when you're facing a penalty kick? Consider: The spot is twelve yards away. The ball is coming at seventy miles an hour. A goalkeeper has a tenth of a second to react.

If you're Alyssa Naeher, you don't wave your arms around to distract the shooter. You don't bounce all over the place. You don't scream smack at your opponent. Instead, you give nothing away while your brain processes every bit of data on the kicker's previous PKs. And then: Boom. You make three heroic stops that send your team to the Olympic semifinals or one monster save that sends your team to the World Cup final without calling any attention to yourself.

But of course, spot kicks hardly sum up the enormous range of Naeher's goalkeeping skills. She reads the opponent's threats; organizes the defensive shape; intercepts crosses, cleans up through-balls, and rebounds; positions set pieces; commands her penalty area; and distributes from the back to spark attacks—all while exuding confidence and composure, a reassuring aura. As someone once said, clean sheets speak louder than words.

FIFA World Cup
Experience:
2015, 2019

Position:
Goalkeeper

Nickname:
Lyss

Height: **5'9"**

Birthdate:
April 20, 1988

Hometown:
Stratford, CT

College:
Penn State

First USWNT Cap:
December 18, 2014

Notable Honors:
**2007 & 2008
NSCAA First-Team
All-American**

FYI:
**Scored more than
2,000 points as a
standout high school
basketball player and
dreamed of playing
at UConn**

Instagram:
alyssanaeher

Twitter:
@AlyssaNaeher

FIFA World Cup Experience:
None

Position:
Forward

Nickname:
Soph

Height: **5'6"**

Birthdate:
August 10, 2000

Hometown:
Windsor, CO

College:
Stanford

First USWNT Cap:
November 27, 2020

Notable Honors:
2018 Pac-12 All-Freshman Team; Most Outstanding Offensive Player, 2019 College Cup; no. 1 overall pick in 2020 NWSL Draft (Portland Thorns)

FYI:
Proud owner of a fish she named Cholula, after her favorite hot sauce

Instagram:
sophsssmith

Twitter:
@_sophsssmith

SOPHIA SMITH

SHE WILL MAKE YOU PAY. If you switch off for a nanosecond. If you play a loose pass in your end. If you underestimate her closing speed.

Do any of those things and the bill will come quickly—and you won't like the grand total you'll see on the scoreboard.

Smith has the predatory instincts of all natural goal scorers: She is always lurking. She can sniff out any chance. She will pop up out of nowhere in the box. And more often than not, the ball's next stop is the back of the net. Right foot, left foot, head, whatever it takes. She has the strength to hold off opponents, the speed to blow past them, and the dribbling skills to induce vertigo in defenders. She is a supreme opportunist who will exploit the smallest opening when the stakes are the biggest.

Put simply, the slightest mistake will cost you.

↑ Defenders better not blink when squaring up to Smith or the next thing they'll see is the back of her jersey.

MEGAN RAPINOE

From the moment Rapinoe rounds a defender, she's thinking several moves ahead and plotting how best to break down an opposing back line.

YOU NEED A GOAL. You need a player who can deliver it. Someone who thrives on pressure. Someone who divines the currents of the match and can bend them to her skill as surely as she possesses the ball at her feet. With calculating cool she will whip a perfect cross or corner onto a teammate's head. She will imperiously stand over a free kick before beating the 'keeper with sheer power or a finely calibrated curler. She will time a run into the box so precisely that she'll meet the pass or rebound and with one swing of her leg, fire it through the fog of defenders and into the back of the net. When everything is on the line, you need a leader with the mental toughness who can step up to the spot and cold-bloodedly bury a penalty kick to win a World Cup and set off an explosion of joy across the land.

You need Pinoe.

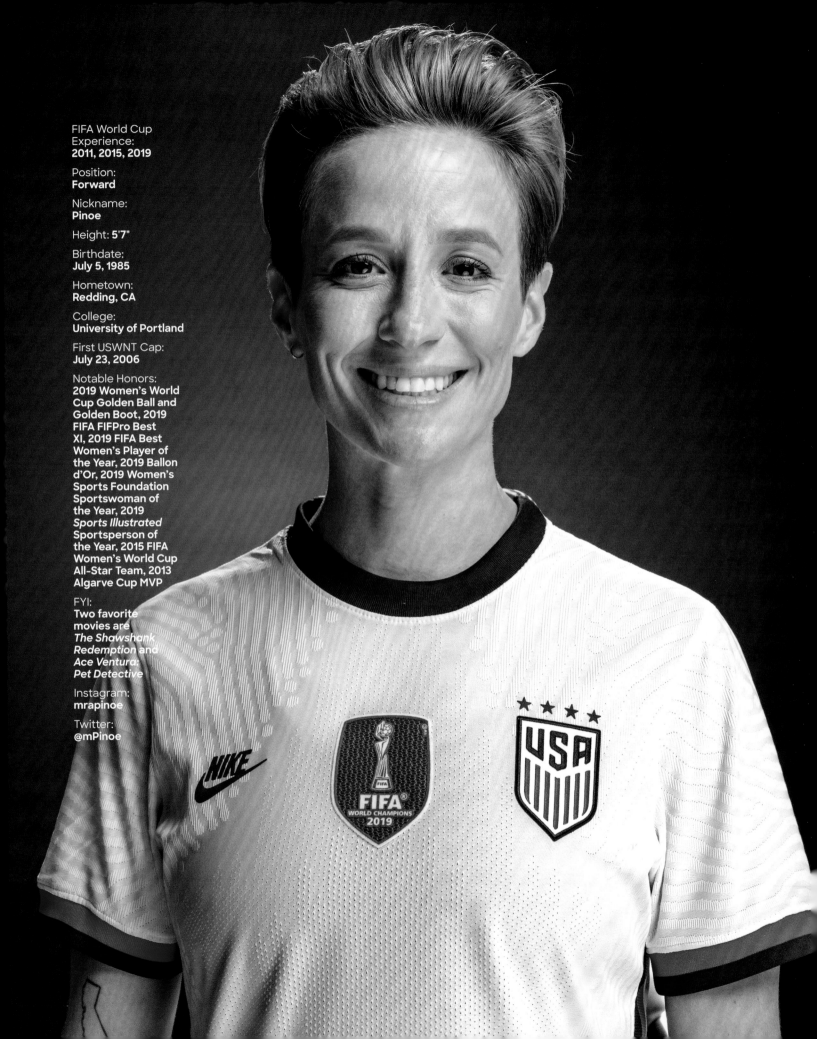

FIFA World Cup
Experience:
2011, 2015, 2019

Position:
Forward

Nickname:
Pinoe

Height: **5'7"**

Birthdate:
July 5, 1985

Hometown:
Redding, CA

College:
University of Portland

First USWNT Cap:
July 23, 2006

Notable Honors:
2019 Women's World Cup Golden Ball and Golden Boot, 2019 FIFA FIFPro Best XI, 2019 FIFA Best Women's Player of the Year, 2019 Ballon d'Or, 2019 Women's Sports Foundation Sportswoman of the Year, 2019 *Sports Illustrated* **Sportsperson of the Year, 2015 FIFA Women's World Cup All-Star Team, 2013 Algarve Cup MVP**

FYI:
Two favorite movies are *The Shawshank Redemption* **and** *Ace Ventura: Pet Detective*

Instagram:
mrapinoe

Twitter:
@mPinoe

JULIE ERTZ

← Even the best forwards in the world, such as Australia's Sam Kerr, can forget about getting to the ball if Ertz has other intentions.

WITH HER PONYTAIL PULLED TAUT, her arms tucked in, and her eyes locked on target, here comes Julie Ertz, and heaven help the opponent who's challenging her for the ball. Thwack. Whomp. Boom. It's a painful lesson that her teammates have learned every day in training: Don't. Go. There. She is "a weapon who will run through anything," according to former USWNT coach Jill Ellis.

An equally fierce and dynamic presence in attack and defense, Ertz patrols from box to box, one second cleaning out opponents and jarring the ball loose, the next, surging downfield and delivering the killer pass.

Without breaking stride, she charges into the penalty area where she fearlessly launches herself headfirst into a chaos of flailing limbs and boots. She may end up playing the rest of the way with a mouthful of bloody gauze. But no matter. Thwack. Whomp. Boom.

FIFA World Cup
Experience:
2015, 2019

Position:
Midfielder

Nickname:
JJ

Height: **5'7"**

Birthdate:
April 6, 1992

Hometown:
Mesa, AZ

College:
Santa Clara University

First USWNT Cap:
June 8, 2015

Notable Honors:
**2017 & 2019 U.S.
Soccer Female
Player of the Year**

FYI:
**First date with future
husband and NFL star
Zach Ertz: Chipotle**

Instagram:
julieertz

Twitter:
@julieertz

FIFA World Cup
Experience:
2011, 2015, 2019

Position:
Defender

Nickname:
Broon

Height: **5'7"**

Birthdate:
June 6, 1985

Hometown:
St. Louis, MO

College:
University of Virginia

First USWNT Cap:
January 16, 2008

Notable Honors:
**2015–2018
CONCACAF Women's
Best XI**

FYI:
**At the 2021
SheBelieves Cup, U.S.
players put names of
inspirational women
on the back of their
jerseys; Sauerbrunn
chose Ruth Bader
Ginsburg and sent
the jersey to the
Supreme Court**

Instagram:
reeba04

Twitter:
@beckysauerbrunn

BECKY SAUERBRUNN

THE OPPOSING STRIKER bears down on goal and shapes to shoot. Except for the U.S. goalkeeper, there is nothing to stop her. Nothing but Becky Sauerbrunn. Measuring her tackle with geometric precision, she leg-whips the ball to safety. She makes the spectacular look routine.

Her teammates may call her "Broon" for short, but her nickname might as well be "Broom." Of course, she does much more than simply sweep aside intruders at the doorstep. Sauerbrunn is the spine, the guts, and the steel of the U.S. backline. She commands and positions her defenders with understated authority. She may be forced to the sideline, she may limp off the field after a hard foul, but she will jump right back into the fray, a model of gritty determination that is the mark of an undaunted leader. Which she emphatically is. She is, after all, the captain.

FIFA World Cup Experience:
2019

Position:
Defender

Nickname:
Scrabbers

Height: **5'7"**

Birthdate:
May 13, 1993

Hometown:
Menlo Park, CA

College:
UCLA

First USWNT Cap:
March 1, 2018

Notable Honors:
2013-14 Honda Award for soccer, 2014 Pac-12 Defender of the Year

FYI:
Played on the same team as Samantha Mewis for 11 consecutive years, four in college at UCLA and seven in the pros with three different teams

Instagram:
abbydahlkemper

Twitter:
@AbbyDahlkemper

YOU DON'T SEE WHAT SHE SEES. What you see is Abby Dahlkemper receiving the ball in her own half from a teammate who surges down the right flank, drawing defenders to her. What Abby sees is the yawning space opening up fifty yards away on the opposite side of the field. What we all see in the next second is a flick of the ankle, a perfectly flighted ball—and the ignition key to the U.S. offense has been turned. It's called switching the point of attack, and no one does it more incisively. Her pass will land softly on the foot of a teammate who appears as not much more than an unreachable speck on the horizon and who will carry that ball into the heart of an unsuspecting defense. Having set the chaos in motion, Dahlkemper will be content to remain behind, staunch and unflappable, a sturdy central pillar of the U.S. defense. Forwards thinking they will go straight through her will receive little joy. She'll see to it.

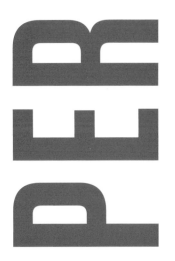

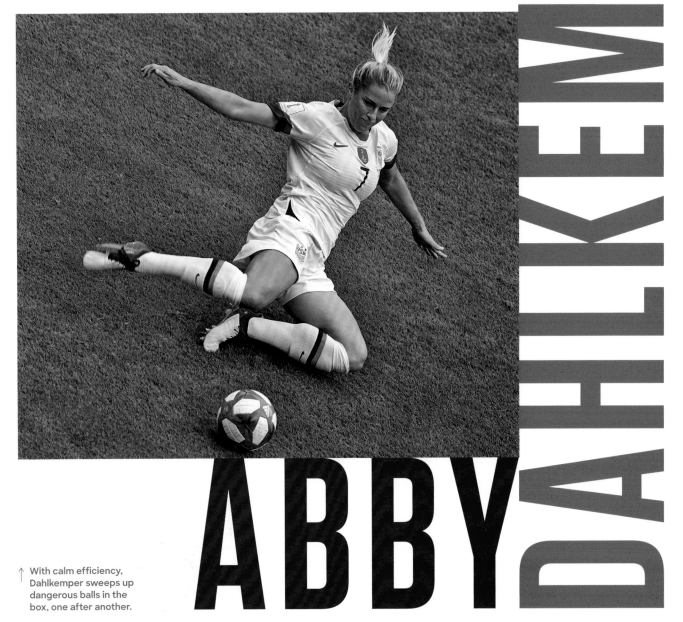

↑ With calm efficiency, Dahlkemper sweeps up dangerous balls in the box, one after another.

ABBY DAHLKEMPER

KELLEY
O'HARA

A blur of constant movement, the inexhaustible O'Hara will do whatever it takes to win the ball.

THERE WILL BE BLOOD. Either hers, a teammate's or an opponent's. That's just the way it's going to be when Kelley O'Hara is on the field. She's a baller's baller, and it doesn't matter if she's hurtling into a 50-50 challenge or an aerial collision—training session, a World Cup final, it makes no difference. She demands to be out there and to hell with the physical toll. How did she transform herself from a high-scoring forward, which she once was, to the nails-hard defender she has become? Pure fearlessness. Her otherwise blithe-spirited demeanor belies a ferocious intensity that won't switch off until she has shut you down and shut you up.

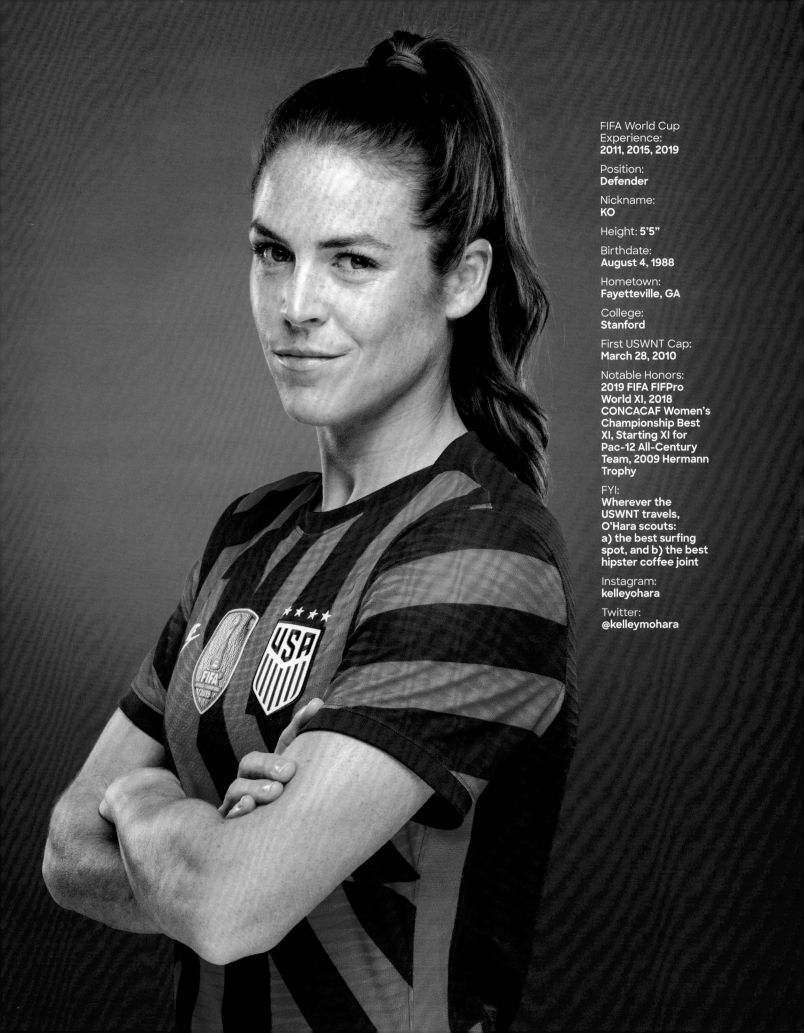

FIFA World Cup
Experience:
2011, 2015, 2019

Position:
Defender

Nickname:
KO

Height: **5'5"**

Birthdate:
August 4, 1988

Hometown:
Fayetteville, GA

College:
Stanford

First USWNT Cap:
March 28, 2010

Notable Honors:
**2019 FIFA FIFPro
World XI, 2018
CONCACAF Women's
Championship Best
XI, Starting XI for
Pac-12 All-Century
Team, 2009 Hermann
Trophy**

FYI:
**Wherever the
USWNT travels,
O'Hara scouts:
a) the best surfing
spot, and b) the best
hipster coffee joint**

Instagram:
kelleyohara

Twitter:
@kelleymohara

ANDI SULLIVAN

FIFA World Cup Experience: **None**

Position: **Midfielder**

Nickname: **Sunny**

Height: **5'7"**

Birthdate: **December 20, 1995**

Hometown: **Lorton, VA**

College: **Stanford**

First USWNT Cap: **October 19, 2016**

Notable Honors: **First overall pick in the 2018 NWSL Draft, 2017 Hermann Award, 2015-17 First-Team All-American; 2016 Pac-12 Player of the Year, 2013 NSCAA Youth Girls' National Player of the Year**

FYI: **At thirteen, she wore banana-yellow cleats and a yellow pinnie to soccer camp, and a nickname was born**

Instagram: **sunnysulli**

Twitter: **@sunshine_sully**

KRISTIE MEWIS

FIFA World Cup Experience: **None**

Position: **Midfielder**

Nickname: **Kratcheeta**

Height: **5'7"**

Birthdate: **February 25, 1991**

Hometown: **Hanson, MA**

College: **Boston College**

First USWNT Cap: **February 9, 2013**

Notable Honors: **2012 NSCAA First-Team All-American; 2012 All-ACC First Team; 2008 FIFA U-17 World Cup Bronze Ball, USSF 2008 Young Female Athlete of the Year**

FYI: **There were 2,722 days between her first and second USWNT goals, most ever for any player**

Instagram: **kmewis19**

Twitter: **@KristieMewie**

MARGARET PURCE

FIFA World Cup Experience: **None**

Position: **Defender**

Nickname: **Midge**

Height: **5'5"**

Birthdate: **September 18, 1995**

Hometown: **Silver Spring, MD**

College: **Harvard**

First USWNT Cap: **November 10, 2019**

Notable Honors: **2015 & 2016 Ivy League Player of the Year; 2016 NSCAA First-Team All-American**

FYI: **Helped start the Black Women's Player Collective in the NWSL**

Instagram: **100purcent**

Twitter: **@100Purcent**

CASEY MURPHY

FIFA World Cup Experience: **None**

Position: **Goalkeeper**

Nickname: **Murph**

Height: **6'1"**

Birthdate: **April 25, 1996**

Hometown: **Bridgewater, NJ**

College: **Rutgers**

First USWNT Cap: **November 27, 2021**

Notable Honors: **2018 NSCAA First-Team All-American; 2018 All-Big Ten First Team; 2018 Big Ten Goalkeeper of the Year**

FYI: **In a November, 2021 friendly against Australia, she became the tallest player ever to earn a cap for the USWNT**

Instagram: **caseymurphy11**

Twitter: **@CaseyMurph**

ASHLEY HATCH

FIFA World Cup Experience: **None**

Position: **Forward**

Nickname: **Ash Smash**

Height: **5'9"**

Birthdate: **May 25, 1995**

Hometown: **Gilbert, AZ**

College: **Brigham Young University**

First USWNT Cap: **October 19, 2016**

Notable Honors: **2018 All-WCC First Team; 2021 NWSL Golden Boot**

FYI: **Hatch donated her goal bonuses from the 2020 NWSL Challenge Cup to the NAACP and DC Cares—organizations that fight racial injustice**

Twitter: **@ash_hatch33**

Instagram: **ash_smash33**

SOFIA HUERTA

FIFA World Cup Experience: **None**

Position: **Defender**

Nickname: **Sof**

Height: **5'6"**

Birthdate: **December 14, 1992**

Hometown: **Boise, ID**

College: **Santa Clara University**

First USWNT Cap: **September 16, 2017**

Notable Honors: **Four-time All-NWSL Second Team; no. 1 overall pick in 2015 NWSL Draft (Chicago Red Stars)**

FYI: **By auctioning off her jersey, cleats, and a twenty-minute FaceTime, she raised more than $15,000 for the Loveland Foundation, which "helps bring opportunity and healing for communities of color"**

Instagram: **sofiahuerta**

Twitter: **@schuerta**

EMILY FOX

FIFA World Cup
Experience: **None**

Position:
Defender

Nickname:
Foxy

Height: **5'5"**

Birthdate:
July 5, 1998

Hometown:
Ashburn, VA

College:
University of North Carolina

First USWNT Cap:
January 19, 2019

Notable Honors:
2018 & 2019 All-ACC First Team; no. 1 overall pick in the 2021 NWSL Draft (Racing Louisville FC)

FYI:
Is an avid reader of fantasy novels

Instagram:
_emilyfox

Twitter:
@_emilyfox

ALANA COOK

FIFA World Cup
Experience: **None**

Position:
Defender

Nickname:
Lans

Height: **5'9"**

Birthdate:
April 11, 1997

Hometown:
Far Hills, NJ

College:
Stanford

First USWNT Cap:
November 10, 2019

Notable Honors:
2018 First-Team All-American; 2018 Pac-12 Defender of the Year

FYI:
Grew up watching Manchester United games from the age of four with her English-born father, but chose to play for the U.S.

Instagram:
alana.cook

Twitter:
@_alana_cook

LYNN WILLIAMS

FIFA World Cup
Experience: **None**

Position:
Forward

Nickname:
Lynnie

Height: **5'7"**

Birthdate:
May 21, 1993

Hometown:
Fresno, CA

College:
Pepperdine

First USWNT Cap:
October 19, 2016

Notable Honors:
2016 NWSL MVP, Golden Boot & Best XI; 2014 NSCAA First-Team All-American; 2012-2014 All-WCC First Team

FYI:
Grew up on a pecan farm in Clovis, CA and would be happy if she never saw a pecan pie for the rest of her life

Instagram:
lynnwilliams9

Twitter:
@lynnraenie

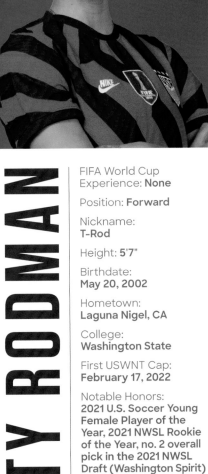

NAOMI GIRMA

FIFA World Cup
Experience: **None**

Position:
Defender

Nickname:
Nay

Height: **5'6"**

Birthdate:
June 14, 2000

Hometown:
San Jose, CA

College:
Stanford

First USWNT Cap:
April 12, 2022

Notable Honors:
No. 1 overall pick in 2022 NWSL Draft (San Diego Wave); 2020 U.S. Soccer Young Female Player of the Year; 2019 NCAA Champion; Captain of U-20 USWNT

FYI:
Began playing in the Bay Area with the Maleda Soccer Club, a gathering of Ethiopian families where the grown-ups barbecued and the kids scrimmaged on the field

Instagram:
naomi_girma

Twitter:
@naomi_girma

TRINITY RODMAN

FIFA World Cup
Experience: **None**

Position: **Forward**

Nickname:
T-Rod

Height: **5'7"**

Birthdate:
May 20, 2002

Hometown:
Laguna Nigel, CA

College:
Washington State

First USWNT Cap:
February 17, 2022

Notable Honors:
2021 U.S. Soccer Young Female Player of the Year, 2021 NWSL Rookie of the Year, no. 2 overall pick in the 2021 NWSL Draft (Washington Spirit)

FYI:
In January, 2022, Rodman signed the richest contract in NWSL history, a four-year, $1.1 million deal, more than her father, Dennis Rodman, made in his first two NBA seasons combined

Instagram:
trinity_rodman

Twitter:
@trinity_rodman

ASHLEY SANCHEZ

FIFA World Cup
Experience: **None**

Position:
Midfielder

Nickname:
Sanchita

Height: **5'4"**

Birthdate:
March 16, 1999

Hometown:
Monrovia, CA

College:
UCLA

First USWNT Cap:
November 27, 2021

Notable Honors:
2019 All-Pac-12 First-Team; 2018 First Team United Soccer Coaches All-American

FYI:
Was the United States flag bearer for the 2019 World University Games in Naples, Italy

Instagram:
ashley.sanchez

Twitter:
None

→
In her unwavering pursuit of greatness, Press radiates pure joy here as she scores against Mexico in 2021.

"In the final third, I think I've always had a goal scorer's mentality," Press says. "Once I'm in shooting range, I don't think about anything else. If I happen to pass, it's because I couldn't shoot. And I think that there's a breed of players that are just wired that way."

JEFF KASSOUF, *The Equalizer*

Kashima, Japan—The bronze medal the United States earned in a 4-3 victory over Australia on Thursday at Ibaraki Kashima Stadium measures 85 millimeters in diameter, weighs less than a pound, and has a lot to say about the Americans, for an inanimate object. Among its statements: 39- and 36-year-olds are not too elderly to win soccer games. The U.S. women's soccer team is still worthy of the world's fear. And isn't this better when we're all having fun?

"Woo!" Megan Rapinoe wailed by way of opening her news conference, complete with a James Brown high kick. "I feel good."

Rapinoe sang like she played Thursday: with joy. She and Carli Lloyd, with two goals apiece, led a rejuvenated U.S. squad to the program's sixth Olympic medal—an achievement that came five years after the team was ousted in the quarterfinals of the 2016 Olympic Games in Rio de Janeiro and three days after it faced the bitter sting of a semifinal loss to Canada.

The U.S. women did so with a balance of fun and intensity that has been missing from an otherwise perplexing and lifeless run through these Games.

"At the end of the day, it's about a mentality that this team has had forever," Lloyd said. "We may look like the most talented team on paper . . . but as we all know, talent doesn't win you championships. And without the mentality, without the heart, the grit, the fight, we won't win anything."

When Lloyd finally stopped running against Australia, subbed off in the 81st minute, she got a high five or swift embrace from every teammate and coach before Rapinoe wrapped her in a bear hug. It was quick. They would have plenty of time for celebration when the game was won, for sentimentality and nostalgia whenever they do decide to retire—a whole lifetime of it, stretching ahead.

AVA WALLACE, *Washington Post*

Earning her first cap against the Czech Republic in the 2022 SheBelieves Cup, Trinity Rodman, the NWSL's Rookie of the Year, displays the speed, touch, and athleticism that has USWNT fans buzzing about her future.

← Following its bitter semifinal loss to Canada in the 2020 Olympics, the U.S. Women convened a players-only meeting in which, according to captain Becky Sauerbrunn, "truths" were aired. Inspired by a renewed resolve, the team rallied to beat Australia for the bronze medal.

What's next? What's next? What's next?

. . . We are at the end of an era of titans playing three hundred-plus matches for their countries—not a bad thing, but certainly something that is unfamiliar at this point. We are at the end of a decade with this version of the USWNT, which truly rose to public consciousness with Megan Rapinoe's left foot connecting with the ball and finding the head of Abby Wambach on a July day in 2011 in Dresden.

It's time to say goodbye to this chapter of the team's history, though. . . . Of course, there's plenty of anticipation for the younger USWNT players to step into more playing time, for incoming talent to start earning more consistent call-ups, for the work of a new cycle to begin. That's the nature of sports—to look to the next big thing. It's also natural to want to set aside the discomfort to fully embrace the anticipation of the next chapter of this team, to start the work because the competition is improving and there is no time to waste. . . .

These days were always coming. This threshold was always waiting—beckoning like a long, empty hallway that hopefully leads to glittering new space.

MEG LINEHAN, *The Athletic*

The U.S. has won a record four World Cup trophies—1991, 1999, 2015, 2019.

OUTSIDE THE LINES

2022: U.S. Soccer and the players' unions for USWNT and USMNT reach a landmark agreement in which the women and men will receive equal pay and split the prize money for their respective World Cups.

On Equal Pay Day, March 15, 2022, Vice President Kamala Harris hosted past and present USWNT players at the White House (left to right): U.S. Soccer President Cindy Parlow Cone, Margaret Purce, Kamala Harris, Briana Scurry, Julie Foudy, and Kelley O'Hara. They led the vice president in a "Oosa Oosa Oosa Uhhhh" cheer and made her an honorary teammate.

CALLING THE SHOTS

1985
MIKE RYAN
0-3-1
Helped kick-start the USWNT program from scratch

1986-1994
ANSON DORRANCE
65-22-5
The 1991 World Cup title was a first for U.S. women or men

1994-1999
TONY DICICCO
105-8-8
Beloved U.S. coach led the 99ers to World Cup glory

2000
LAUREN GREGG
2-0-1
First female USWNT coach served in interim role after DiCicco's departure

2000-2004
APRIL HEINRICHS
87-17-20
World Cup-winning captain in '91 coached 2004 team to Olympic gold

2005-2007
GREG RYAN
45-1-9
Dismissed after his only loss (4-0 to Brazil in 2007 World Cup semifinal), the worst ever suffered by USWNT

2008-2012
PIA SUNDHAGE
91-6-10
Won two Olympic golds and reached World Cup final during her tenure

2012-2014
TOM SERMANNI
18-2-4
Unbeaten in sixteen matches in 2013, but was replaced after seventh-place finish in the 2014 Algarve Cup

2014-2019
JILL ELLIS
106-7-19
En route to two World Cup titles, was undefeated (23-0-1) in WC qualifiers and games

2019-Present
VLATKO ANDONOVSKI
28-2-4*
After bronze medal in the 2020 Olympics, is retooling a deep USWNT roster for World Cup title defense in 2023

Through 2021

THE GREATEST OF ALL-TIME XI

MIA
HAMM

MICHELLE
AKERS

CARLI
LLOYD

ABBY
WAMBACH

KRISTINE
LILLY

BECKY
SAUERBRUNN

JULIE
FOUDY

CHRISTIE
RAMPONE

HOPE
SOLO

CARLA
OVERBECK

JOY
FAWCETT

Selected by a panel of current and former USWNT players, coaches, and members of the media. See page 254.

ACKNOWLEDGMENTS

IF THE PREVAILING ethos of the USWNT is an unwavering refusal to accept anything less than the best of every team member, then the book you hold in your hands reflects that spirit. From the initial kickoff eighteen months ago to the final whistle, everyone involved in this project displayed an enduring commitment, starting with the two women whose names appear on the cover. Julie Foudy and Gwendolyn Oxenham brought their love of the game and their warrior mentality to convey on the page what the U.S. Women experience on the field. We're indebted to the peerless design team of Robert Priest and Grace Lee, who stayed the course despite our countless revisions, not to mention the pandemic, and ultimately produced this elegant tribute. Dorothy McMahon and Carolyn Davis graciously met our unceasing requests for photos, consistently coming up with compelling images. Thanks also to our resident stats guru David Sabino for his deep dives into an ocean of numbers none of us could fathom.

Still, the ball would never have started rolling without Susan Canavan, our agent, who has long been a champion for women's sports. Susan found us the perfect editor in Matt Inman, a longtime fan of women's soccer whose steadfast enthusiasm and exacting attention to detail made this a better book. We are also grateful to Ten Speed's estimable creative director Kelly Booth for her inspired work in the home stretch.

From the outset, USWNT's press officer Aaron Heifetz provided invaluable support and wisdom through endless phone calls, emails and expensive lunches on our dime. His colleagues at U.S. Soccer, Neil Buethe and Mike Gressle, encouraged the project from the very start. Becca Roux, the executive director of the USWNT Players Association, and her indefatigable deputy, Annie Reid, were instrumental in helping us gain the support of the players.

Special thanks to all the writers and photographers whose stellar work graces these pages and particularly to John Todd and Annette Shelby at ISI Photos for opening up their archives to us. And thanks as well to our panel of experts who helped select the All-Decade and All-Time teams (see right, How the Polling Was Done).

We'd like to give a well-deserved shoutout to our families who never once changed the locks on us as we grumpily toiled away at all hours of the day and night. So our heartfelt appreciation to Jan Cherubin, Chloe Director, Susan Squire, Emily Hirshey, Joe and Josh Tracy, Marilyn Johnson, Jackson and Carolyn and Nick Fleder.

And lastly, to the women of the National Team for the inspiration they've provide to millions of young girls (and boys) and for making the history that we hope we've done justice to in these pages.

The Editors
May 30, 2022

Julie Foudy:
Thanks to all the women who have worn the jersey and to all the female pioneers on whose shoulders we have stood, jumped, and done backflips.

Gwen Oxenham:
Thank you to the players for sharing their stories and thank you to my favorite old gents for their constant enthusiasm.

How the Polling Was Done

The voting for the All-Decade and All-Time teams was conducted in partnership with the USWNT Players' Association, which polled current and former National Team players from various eras. The players voted anonymously and their selections were then tabulated alongside those from a panel comprised of coaches, journalists, and broadcasters. We are grateful to the following for their participation:

Pia Sundhage—Coach of Brazil and former coach of USWNT

Anson Dorrance—Coach of University of North Carolina and former coach of USWNT

Emma Hayes—Coach of Chelsea Ladies and FIFA's 2021 Coach of the Year

Alexi Lalas—Former USMNT player and soccer analyst for Fox Sports

JP Dellacamera—Play-by-play announcer for Fox Sports

Jenn Hildreth—Play-by-play announcer for the NWSL on CBS

Grant Wahl—Author of the bestseller *The Beckham Experiment* and former soccer writer for *Sports Illustrated*

Jeff Kassouf—Founder of The Equalizer

Jonathan Tannenwald—Soccer writer, *Philadelphia Inquirer*

Ann Killion—Coauthor of the bestseller *Solo: A Memoir of Hope* and columnist for the *San Francisco Chronicle*

Steph Yang—Soccer writer, *The Athletic*

Kevin Baxter—Soccer writer, *Los Angeles Times*

Wayne Coffey—Coauthor of memoirs by Carli Lloyd and Brianna Scurry

Beau Dure—Regular contributor to *The Guardian* and Soccer America

Ann Peterson—Soccer writer, Associated Press

Suzanne Wrack—Soccer writer, *The Guardian*

Michael Lewis—Soccer historian

Jennifer Cooper—USWNT and NWSL statistics analyst

Paul Carr—Former head of soccer research at ESPN

Paul Kennedy—Editor-in-Chief, Soccer America

Gwen Crooks—Sirius XM Radio

PHOTO CREDITS

COVER

Richard Heathcote/Getty Images **Back Cover** Top from left: George Tiedeman/*Sports Illustrated*/Getty Images; Laurence Griffiths/FIFA/Getty Images; middle from left: David Madison/Getty Images; Shaun Botterill/Getty Images; bottom from left: Brad Smith/ISI Photos; Richard Heathcote/Getty Images

FRONTMATTER

Endpapers Courtesy of players; **2** Xu Zijian Xinhua/eyevine/Redux; **4-5** Alex Grimm/Getty Images; **6-7** Jonathan Ferrey/Getty Images

FOREWORD

9 Joe Faraoni/ESPN Images; **10** Harry How/Getty Images; **11** From top: Michael Pimentel/ISI Photos; Roy K. Miller/ISI Photos; **12** Courtesy Julie Foudy; **13** Lawrence Jackson/Planet Pix/ZUMA Press

1980s

14-15 Courtesy Lisa Gmitter-Pittaro; **16** Courtesy Chiani Design; **16-17** Courtesy US Soccer; **17** Courtesy US Soccer

1990s

18-19 Phil Stephens Photography/FIFA Museum; **20-21** George Tiedemann/*Sports Illustrated*/Getty Images; **23** From top: Will McIntyre/The LIFE Images Collection/Getty Images; Imaginechina/AP Images; **24** Bob Thomas/Getty Images; **25** David E. Klutho/*Sports Illustrated*/Getty Images; **26** Both images: David Madison/Getty Images; **27** Luca Bruno/AP Photo; **28-29** Hector Mata/AFP/Getty Images; **30** John Todd/ISI Photos; **33** J. Brett Whitesell/ISI Photos; **34** Clockwise from top: David Leeds/Allsport/Getty Images; Ron Galella/Getty Images; Mike Powell/Allsport/Getty Images; PA Images/Alamy; **35** All images: ISI Photos; AP Images; Getty Images; **36-37** Robert Beck/*Sports Illustrated*/Getty Images; **38** Bob Thomas/Getty Images; **39** Mike Segar/Reuters; **40** George Tiedemann/*Sports Illustrated*/Getty Images; **41** Bob Thomas/Getty Images; **42** David Madison/Getty

Images; **43** Will McIntyre/The LIFE Images Collection/Getty Images; **44-45** Bob Thomas/Getty Images; **46** David E. Klutho/*Sports Illustrated*/Getty Images; **48** Bob Thomas/Getty Images; **48-49** Gary Hershorn/Reuters; **50** Elsa/Getty Images; **52-56** George Tiedemann/*Sports Illustrated*/Getty Images (3); **57** David Cannon/Allsport/Getty Images; **58** J. Brett Whitesell/ISI Photos; **58-59** Bob Thomas/Getty Images; **60-61** Mike Nelson/AFP/Getty Images; **62** George Tiedemann/*Sports Illustrated*/Getty Images; **63** John W. McDonough/*Sports Illustrated*/Getty Images; **65** David Madison/Getty Images; **66** Pam Whitesell/ISI Photos; **67** Michel Lipchitz/AP Images; **68-69** Jon Buckle/Empics/Getty Images; **71-73** John Todd/ISI Photos (2); **74** Ezra Shaw/Getty Images; **76-77** Peter Read Miller/*Sports Illustrated*/Getty Images; **78-79** Robert Beck/*Sports Illustrated*/Getty Images

2000s

80-81 John Todd/ISI Photos; **82-83** Tommy Hindley/Professional Sport/Popperfoto/Getty Images; **84-85** Henri Szwarc/Bongarts/Getty Images; **85** Brad Smith/ISI Photos; **86** Ben Radford/Getty Images; **87** John Todd/ISI Photos; **88** Shaun Botterill/Getty Images; **89** Michael Pimentel/ISI Photos; **90** Cameron Spencer/Getty Images; **91** Brad Smith/ISI Photos; **92** Armando Franca/AP Images; **93** Brad Smith/ISI Photos; **94** Clockwise from top left: Ben Radford/Getty Images; Bildbyran/ZUMA Press; Richard Drew/AP Images; John Paul Filo/CBS/Getty Images; MediaNews Group/Oakland Tribune/Getty Images; Jamie Squire/Allsport/Getty Images; **95** All images: ISI Photos; **96-97** Ron Cortes/mct/ZUMA Press; **98** Popperfoto/Getty Images; **99** Pam Whitesell/ISI Photos; **100-101** Ezra Shaw/Getty Images; **102** John Todd/ISI Photos; **103** Mark J. Terrill/AP Photo; **104-105** Daniel Garcia/AFP/Getty Images; **105** Kun Ger/Color China Photos/ZUMA Press; **106-107** Odd Andersen/AFP/Getty Images; **108-109** Chung Sung-Jun/Getty Images; **110-11** Tony Quinn/Getty Images;

112-113 Brad Smith/ISI Photos; **114-115** Frederic J. Brown/AFP/Getty Images; **116** Donald Miralle/Getty Images; **117** Marcos Brindicci/Reuters; **118-119** Zhu Gang/AFP/Getty Images; **120** Brad Smith/ISI Photos; **121** Mike Hewitt/ISI Photos; **122-123** Marcos Brindicci/Reuters

2010s

124-125 Laurence Griffiths/FIFA/Getty Images; **126-127** Robert Cianflone/FIFA/Getty Images; **129** Brad Smith/ISI Photos; **130** Andrea Comas/Reuters/Alamy; **131** Jamie Sabau/Getty Images; **132-133** Anthony Bibard/Imago/ZUMA Press; **134** Elsa/Getty Images; **135** Mike Hewitt/FIFA/Getty Images; **136** Bernadett Szabo/Reuters/Alamy; **137** Vi-Images/Hollandse-Hoogte/ZUMA Press; **138** Richard Heathcote/Getty Images; **139** Lucy Nicholson/Reuters/Alamy; **140** From top: Odd Andersen/AFP/Getty Images; Adam Taylor/Disney/Getty Images; Kevin Mazur/LP5/WireImage/Getty Images; **141** All images ISI Photos; **142-143** Elsa/Getty Images; **145** Trent Davol/ISI Photos; **146-147** Thomas Eisenhuth/ISI Photos; **148** Kevin C. Cox/FIFA/Getty Images; **149** Andrew Yates/AFP/Getty Images; **150-151** Deanne Fitzmaurice; **152** Brad Smith/ISI Photos; **153** Stephen Brashear/ISI Photos; **154-155** Doug Pensinger/Getty Images; **156** Thomas Peter/Reuters/Alamy; **156-157** Robert Michael/AFP/Getty Images; **158-159** Both images Chuck Myers/Tribune News Service/Getty Images; **160-161** Brad Smith/ISI Photos; **162-163** Franck Fife/AFP/Getty Images; **164** Popperfoto/Getty Images; **165** David Bernal/ISI Photos; **166-167** Steven Limentani/ISI Photos; **168** Brad Smith/ISI Photos; **169** Dennis Grombkowski/Bongarts/Getty Images; **170-171** Steven Limentani/ISI Photos; **172-173** Mike Hewitt/FIFA/Getty Images; **175** John Todd/ISI Photos; **176** Catherine Ivill/FIFA/Getty Images; **176-177** Quality Sport Images/Getty Images; **178** Brad Smith/ISI Photos; **179** Quality Sport Images/Getty Images; **180** Robert Cianflone/Getty Images; **181** Alex Caparros/

FIFA/Getty Images; **182** VI Images/Getty Images; **182-183** Quality Sport Images/Getty Images; **184-185** Alex Grimm/Getty Images; **186** Catherine Ivill/FIFA/Getty Images; **187** Franck Fife/AFP/Getty Images; **188-189** Benoit Tessier/Reuters/Alamy; **191** Catherine Ivill/FIFA/Getty Images; **192-193** Richard Heathcote/Getty Images; **194-195** Maddie Meyer/FIFA/Getty Images

2020s

196-200 Brad Smith/ISI Photos (3); **201** From left: Michael Regan/FIFA/Getty Images; Courtesy U.S. Soccer; Brad Smith/ISI Photos; **202** Jonathan Moscrop/Getty Images; **203** Robert Mora/ISI Photos; **204** Tim Nwachukwu/Getty Images; **205** From top: Al Chang/Stanford Athletics/ISI Photos; Brad Smith/ISI Photos; **206** Brad Smith/ISI Photos; **207** Courtesy U.S. Soccer; **208** Roy K. Miller/ISI Photos; **209** Dennis Schneidler/*USA Today Sports*/Reuters; **210** Howard Smith/ISI Photos; **211-212** Brad Smith/ISI Photos (2); **213** Zhizhao Wu/Getty Images; **214** Cory Knowlton/ZUMA Press; 215 John Todd/ISI Photos; **216-218** Brad Smith/ISI Photos (4); **219** Roy K. Miller/ISI Photos; **220-221** Both images Brad Smith/ISI Photos; **222** Daniela Porcelli/ISI Photos; **223-225** Brad Smith/ISI Photos (3); **226** Mark Smith/ZUMA Press; 227 Roy K. Miller/ISI Photos; **228-229** Brad Smith/ISI Photos (2); **230** Dean Mouhtaropoulos/Getty Images; **231-233** Brad Smith/ISI Photos (3); **234** Tim Clayton/Corbis/Getty Images; **235** Brad Smith/ISI Photos; **236** Livemedia/IPA/ZUMA Press; **237-239** Brad Smith/ISI Photos (3); **240** John Todd/ISI Photos; **241** Quality Sport Images/Getty Images; **242-247** All images Brad Smith/ISI Photos; **248-249** Howard Smith/ISI Photos; **250** Naomi Baker/Getty Images; **251** Brad Smith/ISI Photos; **252** Top left: Courtesy National Soccer Hall of Fame, Frisco, TX; Top right: White House Photo; Bottom rows: first on left, Courtesy Frank MacDonald; others, ISI Photos; **253** All images: Getty Images; ISI Photos; Alamy

Typefaces: Letters from Sweden's Ivar Text, Sharp Type's Sharp Sans,
Hoefler & Co.'s Tungsten, and Lineto GmbH's Alpha Headline

Grateful acknowledgment is made to the following sources for the permission to reprint these excerpts. Some excerpts have been condensed and edited for clarity. **1990s:** 38 Kieran Theivam & Jeff Kassouf/Robinson; 39 Gemma Clarke/Bold Type Books; 41 *The Girls of Summer: The U.S. Women's Soccer Team and How it Changed the World* by Jeré Longman. © 2000 by Jeré Longman. Used by permission of HarperCollins Publishers; 41 Caitlin Murray/Abrams Press; 43 Gary Smith/*Sports Illustrated*; 43 Tim Nash; 45 From *The New York Times*. © 1991 The New York Times Company. All rights reserved. Used under license; 47 Alex Abnos/*Sports Illustrated*; 48 Kieran Theivam & Jeff Kassouf/Robinson; 49 Holly Brubach/From *The New York Times*. © 1996 The New York Times Company. All rights reserved. Used under license; 51 Tim Nash; 51 Sam Walker/Random House; 53 Mia Hamm/Dey St./It Books; 54 Johnette Howard/*ESPN*; 56 Mike Penner/*Los Angeles Times*; 56 Jeré Longman/*The New York Times*; 58 Michael Farber/*Sports Illustrated*; 61 David Hirshey/*ESPN*; 62 Jeff Bradley/*Sports Illustrated*; 63 Caitlin Dewey/*Washington Post*; 64 Gary Smith/*Sports Illustrated*; 67 Bonnie DiSimone; *Chicago Tribune*; 69-70 *The Girls of Summer: The U.S. Women's Soccer Team and How it Changed the World* by Jeré Longman. © 2000 by Jeré Longman. Used by permission of HarperCollins Publishers (2); 73 Grant Wahl/*Sports Illustrated*; 75 Gary Smith/*Sports Illustrated*; Mia Hamm/Dey St./It Books; 78 Gwen Knapp/*San Francisco Examiner* **2000s:** 99 Tim Nash; 99 NBC Universal; 100 *The Girls of Summer: The U.S. Women's Soccer Team and How it Changed the World* by Jeré Longman. © 2000 by Jeré Longman. Used by permission of HarperCollins Publishers; 102 Tim Nash; 102 *I'm Home*, Shannon Boxx/*The Players' Tribune*; 104 Hon. Fred Upton/Congressional Record; 105 Melissa Segura/*Sports Illustrated*; 106 Tyler Kepner/From *The New York Times*. © 2004 The New York Times Company. All rights reserved. Used under license; 109 Wayne Coffey/*New York Daily News;* 110 Hope Solo with Ann Killion/HarperCollins; 114 Jeré Longman/From *The New York Times*. © 2007 The New York Times Company. All rights reserved. Used under license; 116 Abby Wambach/Dey St.; 117 Angela Hulces/U.S. Soccer; 120 Lucas Shaw and Philip Hersh/*Los Angeles Times*; 121 © *Los Angeles Times*; 122 Carli Lloyd with Wayne Coffey/Houghton Mifflin Harcourt **2010s:** 143 © *Eight by Eight* magazine; 143 Suzanne Wrack/*The Guardian*; 144 Ann Killion/*Sports Illustrated*; 146 Gwendolyn Oxenham/*Sports Illustrated*; 148 David Hirshey/*ESPN*; 149 Alyssa Roenigk/*ESPN*; 150 Patrick Cohn; 152 *The Pursuit*, Christen Press/*The Players' Tribune*; 153 Graham Hays/*ESPN*; 154 Ramona Shelburne/*ESPN*; 156 *The Cross*, Megan Rapinoe/*The Players' Tribune*; 157 Abby Wambach/Dey St.; 158 Mark Zeigler/*San Diego Tribune*; 159 Sally Jenkins/From *Washington Post*. © 2012 *Washington Post*. All rights reserved. Used under license. 161 Grant Wahl/Sports Illustrated; 162 Gwendolyn Oxenham/U.S. Soccer; 164 Louisa Thomas/Grantland.com/ESPN Internet Ventures; 165 Grant Wahl/*Sports Illustrated*; 166 Brian Phillips/Grantland.com/ESPN Internet Ventures; 168 Liviu Bird/*Sports Illustrated*; 169 Allison McCann/Grantland.com/ESPN Internet Ventures; 171 Grant Wahl/*Sports Illustrated*; 173 Hallie Grossman/*ESPN The Magazine*; 174 Hillary Rodham Clinton & Chelsea Clinton/Simon & Schuster; 176 © The Jon Gordon Companies, Inc.; 177 *Snacks with Lynn & Sam*/© 2022 Just Women's Sports; 179 Ann Killion/From *San Francisco Chronicle*. © 2018 Hearst Newspapers. All rights reserved. Used under license; 179 Eric Betts/*Slate*; 180 Meg Linehan/The Athletic; 181 Jamele Hill/*The Atlantic*; 182 Neil Morris/The Equalizer; 183 Mina Kimes/*ESPN The Magazine*; 184 Jenny Vrentas/*Sports Illustrated*; 186 Graham Hays/*ESPN*; 187 Franklin Foer/*The Atlantic*; 188, 193 Rory Smith/From *The New York Times*. © 2019 The New York Times Company. All rights reserved. Used under license; 195 Brian Phillips/The Ringer **2020s:** 248 Jeff Kassouf/*Equalizer Magazine*; 250 Ava Wallace/From *Washington Post*. © 2021 *Washington Post*. All rights reserved. Used under license; 251 Meg Linehan/The Athletic

Library of Congress Cataloging-in-Publication Data is on file with the publisher.

Hardcover ISBN: 978-1-9848-6084-2
eBook ISBN: 978-1-9848-6085-9

Printed in China

Acquiring editor: Matt Inman | Production editor: Leigh Saffold | Editorial assistant: Fariza Hawke
Designer: Priest & Grace | Design manager: Kelly Booth | Production designer: Mari Gill
Production manager: Jane Chinn| Prepress color managers: Neil Spitkovsky and
Nick Patton | Retoucher: Claudia Sanchez
Photography editors: Dot McMahon and Carolyn E. Davis
Data and Statistics: David Sabino | Proofreader: Jeff Campbell
Publicist: Kristin Casemore | Marketer: Allison Renzulli

10 9 8 7 6 5 4 3 2 1

First Edition

Julie Foudy is a former captain of the U.S. Women's Soccer Team, and two-time Olympic gold medalist and World Cup champion. She is currently an on-air reporter and analyst for ESPN, espnW, and ABC. She is host of ESPN's *Laughter Permitted* podcast, and a founding co-owner of the Angel City Football Club.

Gwendolyn Oxenham is the creator of the audio docuseries *Hustle Rule*—hosted by *Ted Lasso*'s Hannah Waddingham—which is based on her book *Under the Lights and in the Dark: Untold Stories of Women's Soccer*. She also wrote *Finding the Game: Three Years, Twenty-five Countries, and the Search for Pickup Soccer* and co-directed *Pelada*, an award-winning documentary about pickup games across the world. A former Duke captain, she played for Brazil's Santos Futebol Clube.

Front endpaper

Back endpaper

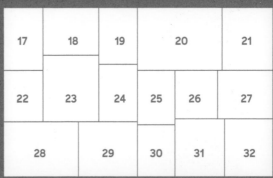

01 Carla Overbeck	09 Tiffany Roberts
02 Tierna Davidson	10 Hope Solo
03 Mia Hamm	11 Catarina Macario
04 Alex Morgan	12 Emily Fox
05 Julie Foudy	13 Sophia Smith
06 Mallory Pugh	14 Andi Sullivan
07 Kelley O'Hara	15 Kristine Lilly
08 Abby Dahlkemper	16 Christie Pearce (Rampone)

17 Trinity Rodman	25 Heather O'Reilly
18 Angela Hucles	26 Rachel Buehler (Van Hollebeke)
19 Amy Rodriguez	27 Samantha and Kristie Mewis
20 Casey Murphy	28 Briana Scurry
21 Heather Mitts	29 Brandi Chastain
22 Carli Lloyd	30 Ashley Sanchez
23 Megan Rapinoe	31 Abby Wambach
24 Ashley Hatch	32 Shannon Boxx